D0607725

Love Letters

Responding to Children in Pain

Love Letters

Responding to Children in Pain

Doris Sanford
Designed by Graci Evans

MULTNOMAH

Portland, Oregon 97266

Unless otherwise indicated, all Scripture references are from the Holy Bible: New International Version, copyright 1973, 1978, 1984 by the International Bible Society. Used by permission of Zondervan Bible Publishers.

Scripture references marked TLB are from The Living Bible, copyright 1971 by Tyndale House Publishers, Wheaton, Ill. Used by permission.

Cover design by Durand Demlow

LOVE LETTERS
©1991 A Corner of the Heart
Published by Multnomah Press
10209 SE Division Street
Portland, Oregon 97266

Multnomah Press is a ministry of Multnomah School of the Bible, 8435 NE Glisan Street, Portland, Oregon 97220.

Printed in the United States of America.

All rights reserved. No part of this publication may be reproduced, stored in a retrieval system, or transmitted, in any form or by any means, electronic, mechanical, photocopying, recording, or otherwise, without the prior written permission of the publisher.

Library of Congress Cataloging-in-Publication Data

Sanford, Doris.
    Love letters : responding to children in pain / Doris Sanford : illustrations by Graci Evans and the children.
        p. cm.
        ISBN 0-88070-435-7
        1. Suffering in children.   2. Children—Correspondence.   3. Sanford, Doris—Correspondence.   4. Suffering—Religious aspects—Christianity.   I. Title.
BF723.S78S26   1991
305.23—dc20   91-25379
                                                                                                        CIP

91 92 93 94 95 96 97 98 99 - 10 9 8 7 6 5 4 3 2 1

Other Books by Doris Sanford and Graci Evans

HURTS OF CHILDHOOD SERIES
This series was developed to offer help and hope to children who have experienced deep and tragic hurts. The books deal gently and compassionately with children's delicate feelings when they're forced to handle burdens far too big for them to carry.

Ages 5-11

IT MUST HURT A LOT
A Child's Book about Death

PLEASE COME HOME
A Child's Book about Divorce

I CAN'T TALK ABOUT IT
A Child's Book about Sexual Abuse

DON'T LOOK AT ME
A Child's Book about Feeling Different

I KNOW THE WORLD'S WORST SECRET
A Child's Book about Living With an Alcoholic Parent

I CAN SAY NO
A Child's Book about Drug Abuse

DON'T MAKE ME GO BACK, MOMMY
A Child's Book about Ritual Abuse

IN OUR NEIGHBORHOOD SERIES
This series for young children addresses problems that might be found in any neighborhood. Each book is written from a child's point of view, expressing the thoughts and emotions of the main character.

Ages 5-11

MARIA'S GRANDMA GETS MIXED UP
BRIAN WAS ADOPTED
LISA'S PARENTS FIGHT
DAVID HAS AIDS

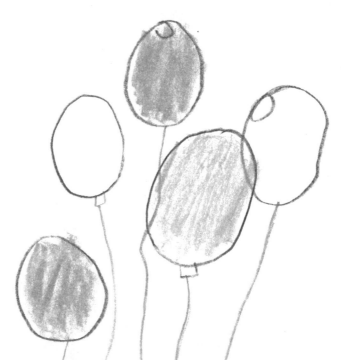

Dedicated with love from Doris to Sharon and Shep Earl
and from Graci to Recie and Tom Raley

Contents

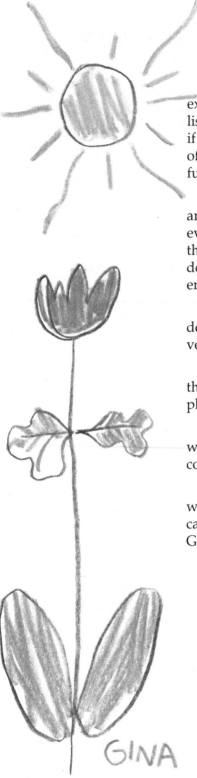

Listening with the Heart

Five years ago we wrote and illustrated a series of books for children who had experienced a major hurt in life. Because we were naive, and maybe because we were listening to God, we added a note on the last page which invited children to write to us if they had no one to talk to about what had happened to them. We received thousands of letters. Some made us smile, some made us cry. All were taken seriously. The letters, full of misspelled words, were brief, to the point, and powerful.

Each child who wrote to us received a personal "love letter" in reply. More than answering unanswerable questions, more than providing information, or direction, or even support, we wanted children to feel loved. We hoped that our loving would give them courage to risk telling their stories again to someone nearby. If they were unable to do that, then we hoped that for a brief moment they would sense that someone had entered their world to stand with them.

None of these hurts of childhood could be cured with one letter. We had no delusions of grandeur. But for many children, this attempt to reach out was a first and very important step. We wanted to honor that step with tenderness and respect.

Our office walls are covered with pictures of children we have never seen. Some of them phone us. A number have adopted us and write us regularly from one foster placement after another. We are honored to be the family that stays put in their lives.

In this book, we are sharing a few of these letters with you. We hope you will listen with your heart, and that our responses to them will provide an example of one way to comfort these tiny wounded. Their names and towns have, of course, been changed.

God gives each of us gifts. We have asked him for the gift of tender hearts. A verse which guides our work is: "We were as gentle among you as a mother feeding and caring for her own children. We loved you dearly—so dearly that we gave you not only God's message, but our own lives too" (1 Thessalonians 2:7-8, TLB).

For them and for him,

Doris Sanford
Graci Evans

Heart to Heart

Heart to Heart

TO GRACI AND DORIS

I'm A girl who needs Help about sex abuse. When I was a child my brother abused me. My dad beats me when he is drunk. from Ty write back?

This is
a picher
of Doris
writing love
letters.

anya
8 years.

Dear Family Member,

Some of you watched helplessly as your child suffered. You longed with all your heart to stop the pain. You would gladly exchange places with your child if only you could.

And some of you have CAUSED the hurt to your child. You never really meant that to happen. It just did, and now your pain is beyond human description. You would give anything to be able to rewrite those chapters, if only . . .

Some of you are grandparents. You knew it was happening and yet each time you hinted or implied or "said it like it was" you were shut out. You've been afraid to risk losing them all, but your life is a living nightmare.

And some are yourselves the wounded children. Your body has grown up but the hurt has never healed. Your past pain is alive and well, and it has wreaked havoc with your relationships, your self-worth, your concept of God, and your ability to maintain intimacy with others. Your childhood pain has touched every corner of your adult life, and you wonder now if it will ever stop.

Our hearts and love and prayers go out to you. Corrie ten Boom said, "There is no pit so deep that God is not deeper still." Remember that when you think you can't hang on any longer.

Our love,

Doris Sanford
Graci Evans

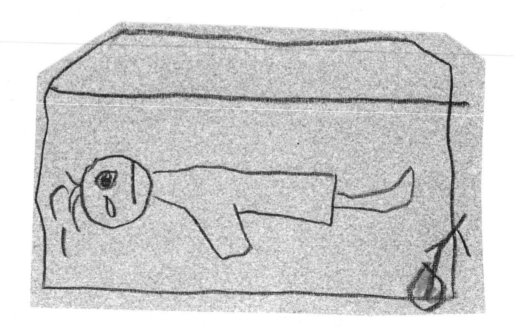

"Gone Forever"
THE GRIEVING CHILD

KE

Children and Grief

Adults can't protect children from loss. Every child experiences some loss.

Grief is the feeling that accompanies loss. All children grieve, even babies.

Children are not short adults—they grieve in ways unique to children.

Children can learn how to manage their losses from seeing adults who don't hide or stuff their pain but are willing to expose it to others.

The more children are included in the family sadness, the easier it will be for them to tolerate suffering. If they are sent to care providers for long periods because "everybody is so upset at home," children are made to bear the pain alone.

Children can only handle "bits and pieces" of grief at a time. They need to step outside of their pain and take time to play.

Children make generalizations, so if a parent dies at the hospital, they assume all people who go to hospitals die.

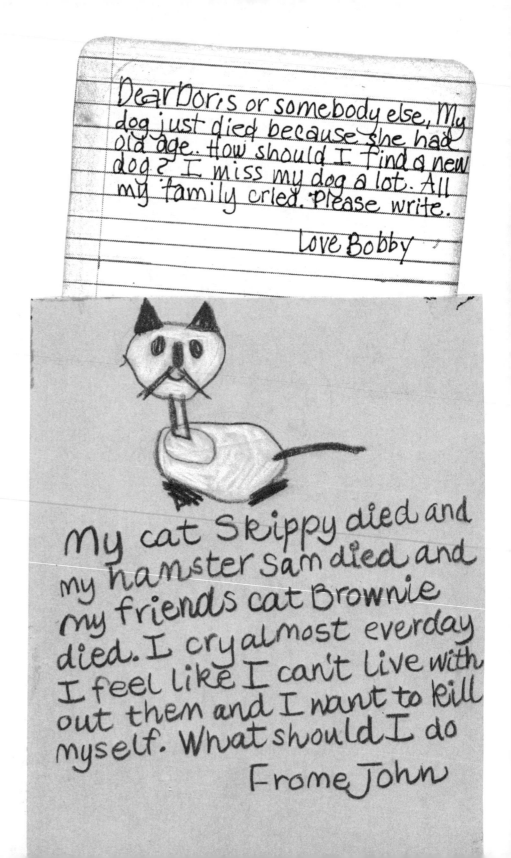

Dear Doris or somebody else, My dog just died because she had old age. How should I find a new dog? I miss my dog a lot. All my family cried. Please write.

Love Bobby

My cat Skippy died and my hamster Sam died and my friends cat Brownie died. I cry almost everday I feel like I can't live with out them and I want to kill myself. What should I do

Frome John

Heart to Heart

Dear John,

What a sad letter you wrote! I am sorry that Skippy, Sam, and Brownie died. Your pets were special friends to you and I know you must feel very, very sad. Sometimes other people don't understand how much you loved your pets and how hard it has been to lose them. It will help to tell them how you feel inside.

Some children say it helped to write a story about their pet. You could tell the story of how they came to live at your house, what you liked best about them, and some of the cute things they did. Remember, John, that the good memories will always be with you. Your little friends were very lucky to have you. I bet they liked you a lot, too!

The sad feelings inside sometimes take a long time to go away. It's OK to cry and let the sadness "spill out." And, when you are happy again, it doesn't mean you have forgotten them.

Love,

Doris

P.S. When I was ten years old I lived on a farm and had thirteen cats, and I loved them all.

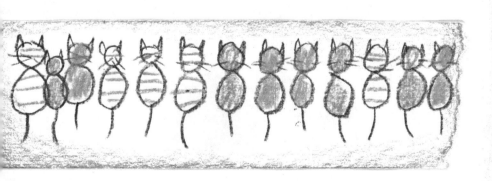

How Children Feel

Children mourn differently: some cry, some don't. Some "act out" their pain, others withdraw and become quiet. All can be equally sad. Children will do what feels best to them to do.

Children release their grief with their bodies: through nightmares, tummy aches, headaches, and loss of appetite.

Not all of the child's feelings will make sense to the adult.

Children in deep mourning still laugh, play, and have fun.

Common grief feelings include guilt, sadness, fear, and confusion.

Children may also feel angry about the death. If so, they often lash out at their siblings.

Children sometimes feel they may have caused the death. They should be told that their angry thoughts didn't cause the person to die; i.e., all children get angry, but anger doesn't make a person die.

It helps children to know what other grieving children feel: this gives children permission to express what they feel.

Understanding Behavior

Hard, simple, physical play releases the pain.

To understand the young child's experience of grief, the adult must enter the world of his play by letting the child select the toys and play experiences. (Children are smarter than adults about play—they know what they need to do.)

When children draw, they will tell their "story" in the art they produce.

Children do not have words for their feelings. What the child does with his behavior IS how he feels.

Children who act angry are often covering up their fear.

Children in grief often act clingy and immature. They are acting in ways that felt secure when they were younger: bed-wetting, tantrums, etc.

Naughty behavior may result from feelings of guilt and the need to be punished.

Trouble at school academically can come from the child's inability to concentrate.

Children can use correct words about death long before they understand their meaning.

Dear Heart to Heart
My Grandma and my Grandpa died. Why? Why? I yelled when there was shooting and it was all my fault. I was one year old. My aunt and uncle died in the WAR too. My monkey pet got killed.

Well, I'm 10 and my father died when I was 7. I never did understand why this happen to me? Why did he leave me so soon? Can you tell me?

Always Christy

Dear Doris,
My name is Michell. I am 7 years old. I want to tell you my DaDDy died six days Ago. Why does God let people my Daddy die?

Love, Michell.

Dear Kai,

I am so glad you wrote and told us a little about what has happened to you. You have had so many losses, and I know you feel deeply sad inside. I'm glad you have talked with your mother about how you feel. It helps the pain to go away a little to tell someone how you feel. It would be easy to ask, "Why did this happen to me?" In the Bible, God's special letter to us, it says that someday when we are in heaven, He will answer all of our questions.

You said that it was your fault that your family died in the war when you were one year old. Dear Kai, would you look at a one-year-old baby very soon and see how tiny and helpless a one-year-old is? Babies cry when they are frightened. They can't help it. They are too young.

God knows none of this was your fault. You were too little, and I bet you were scared. God loves you so much and says you are precious and honored.

Love,

Heart to Heart

Dear Christie,

It was good to get a letter from you. Thank you for telling me what happened in your family. I know it has been hard for you that your dad died, and you miss him very much. Sometimes as kids get a little older they understand more about how their parent's death affected them, and then they feel sad again. You know more now at ten years than you did at seven years about what it means not to have a daddy.

You asked why your dad died. I don't know the answer to that question. It must seem very unfair to you. I do know that the good memories that you have of your dad will never go away and that you can be the kind of girl your dad would be proud of.

Love,

Doris

Explaining Death

Talk about death before a significant loss occurs; e.g., point out a dead bird, take children to a cemetery.

Tell them death is natural, and usually happens when a person is old.

Tell children the exact cause of death.

Children are often unable to know the full meaning of death until they are nine or ten years old. They can be told that the body was the "house" that the person lived in. They can see that the "real person" is gone when they view the body.

Give simple, factual information and then let the children ask what they need to know. Explaining what will no longer be possible for the person who died is sometimes more helpful than explaining what death is, i.e. "Grandma won't eat or talk or move."

Don't tell children the person is happy in heaven without explaining people's tears. Tell them: "We know Grandma is happy, but we miss her very much."

Read stories to them about other children who have experienced loss. It helps to know that their feelings are "normal."

Tell them who their caregivers would be if they were to lose both parents. Children worry about what will happen to them if both parents die.

Talk with them about the death when you are able to focus on their needs. Children are frightened by adults who are hysterical.

What to Avoid

Don't use flowery, philosophical language to talk about the death; e.g., Grandpa didn't "pass away"— he "died."

Don't try to rescue the child from the hurt. Not talking about it just keeps the tears locked inside.

Don't try to make the child feel good about the death; e.g., "Aren't you glad Mommy doesn't hurt anymore?"

Don't underestimate the extent of the child's pain.

Don't assume that because children are young, they won't grieve. Younger children have fewer resources for coping with their pain.

Don't be afraid of losing control or crying in front of the child. Your tears give the child permission to be real.

Don't say to a little boy, "Now you're the man of the house." This lays an unbearable burden on shoulders that are too small for such a load.

Don't quickly replace a pet that dies. Let the child grieve.

Don't give the child all the information about the death in one session. Answer only what the child asks.

I am 9 years old and my litte brother got killed by a moter cycle just like what was in your book" it Must HURT aLot." The secret's in there was mostly true. Exspecially when Eric says QuiT Being a BABY! He was only a dog. My big brother said Quit being a BABY! We went to the Hospital and he had tubes all over. Our family was all there and crying. Matt died. He looked like he was sleeping. I don't know what to do. ~~Coul~~ Could you give me some advice?

your Friend,
Molly

Heart to Heart

Dear Sweet Molly,

Your precious letter came, and I am so glad you wrote. You explained your feelings very well, and that helped us understand what is happening inside you since Matt died.

I have some suggestions that might help you:

1. Talk about your feelings over and over.

2. Don't be afraid to cry. It helps.

3. Some kids feel angry with other people and get into arguments easily. You may want to be by yourself a little more while you are hurting so much.

4. Make a special place where you can go and think about Matt: it might be the cemetery or a spot at your house or yard.

5. Christmas may be a very, very hard time for you because you'll be missing Matt.

6. Lots of kids get tummy aches or have nightmares when they have lost somebody they love. Your body is sad, too.

7. Your mom and dad and brother will be hurting very much, but everybody will show it differently.

God knows all about how much you are hurting and He loves you. You can talk to Him anytime and He will listen. When you get to heaven you can ask God why Matt was killed and He will tell you. (I know it doesn't make any sense now.) The Bible tells us that God's children will see their loved ones again.

I've given you some verses from the Bible that tell about heaven.

If you ever want to write again, I would be so glad to hear from you and will always answer.

I am praying for you, Molly, and I send my love.

Your friend,

Doris

What to Do and Say

Show grieving children you love them. Usually professionals aren't necessary if children are supported by caring adults.

Let children decide whether they will go to the funeral. Tell them what to expect at the service, so they can make a good decision. (If they choose to go, have them sit next to an adult willing to take them out if they want to leave.)

When children ask why, it's okay to respond with, "I don't know."

Save something that belonged to the person who died and give it to the child, e.g., a collection, sweatshirt, etc.

If possible, make a recording of the voice of the person who is dying to give to the child; include stories, messages of love.

Give children something to do to combat their feelings of helplessness; e.g., plant a memory tree or pick flowers for the grave.

Ask if they want to place a toy in the casket as a parting gift.

Maintain structure and limits—regular meals and nap-times should continue. This provides security.

Comfort children by touching, holding, and rocking them.

Mention the name of the person who died often, and keep the child's memories alive.

How Long Do Children Grieve?

Factors which affect the length of grief include:

♡ how close the child was to the person who died. The closer a child is to the person, the longer the grieving process.

♡ the amount of warning the child had of the impending death. If the death was sudden or unexplained the healing process takes longer.

♡ the child's age. Tiny children do not comprehend the extent of their loss and may grieve again as they mature through each developmental stage.

♡ the child's adult role models: whether they are able to provide the support needed.

The loss itself doesn't determine whether the death will leave emotional scars. Most children are self-healing if they are provided a climate of love, acceptance, and security while they do the hard, hard work of mourning.

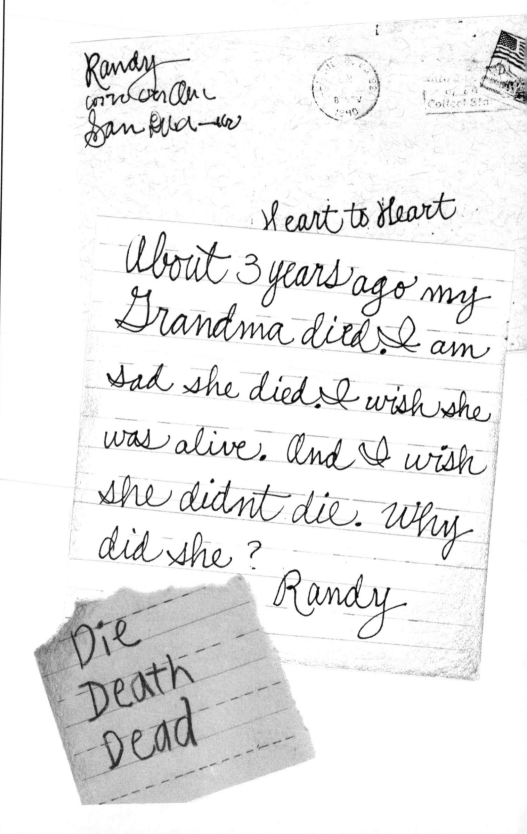

Heart to Heart

About 3 years ago my Grandma died. I am sad she died. I wish she was alive. And I wish she didnt die. Why did she?

Randy

Die
Death
Dead

Heart to Heart

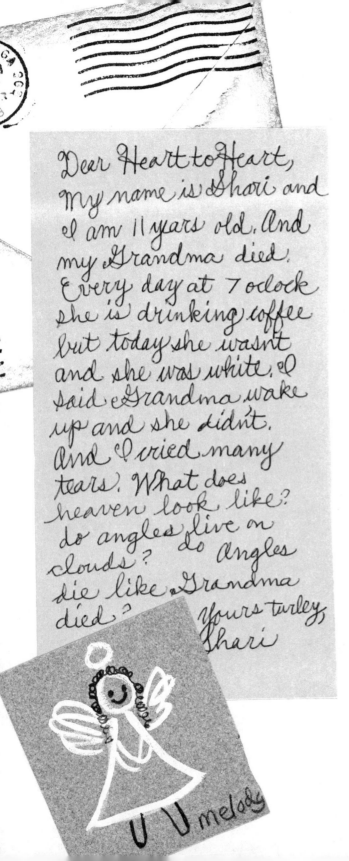

Dear Heart to Heart,
My name is Shari and
I am 11 years old. And
my Grandma died.
Every day at 7 o'clock
she is drinking coffee
but today she wasn't
and she was white. I
said Grandma wake
up and she didn't.
And I cried many
tears. What does
heaven look like?
do angles live on
clouds? do Angles
die like Grandma
died? Yours turley,
Shari

U U melody

Hello Dear Shari,

Thank you for telling me about what happened when your grandma died. It must have been very scary for you and I'm sure you feel sad and miss her very much. She was lucky to have had such a special granddaughter.

I understand why you want to know more about heaven! I am sending some Bible verses that describe heaven. It is a wonderful, wonderful place that God has prepared for people who love Him.

You asked if angels live on clouds. Angels are real and are messengers for God. The Bible says they worship and serve Him around the throne in heaven. They also work as guardian angels for God's children here on earth to protect us from danger. Sometimes angels were visible (when they sang at Jesus' birth) and sometimes they are invisible (when they are guardian angels). I think angels are too busy to sit around on clouds!

You asked if angels die. The answer is no. When we get to heaven there won't be any more death. Not angels, not people. We will live forever with God.

Love and hugs,

Doris

Hello My Name is Katie
I have a grandfather
that will probely die. he
was in a bad accident.
I feel very bad about
it too. I dont think
I can face my grand
mother without a
big cry. It is very
hard because they
live at my home,
could you give me
more information
on Death and heaven.
    KATIE

Dear Heart To Heart
I'm 10 years old. My
name is ERIN. My
ant Ruth was killed
by a horse. We are
having a hard time
dealing with death.
Can you send me some
information about heaven
that might help. ERIN

ERIN

Heart To Heart

HEAVEN

Here are some promises about heaven from the Bible. There are many more, but this is a start:

God will wipe every tear from their eyes. There will be no more sadness, crying or pain (see Revelation 7:17).

Those people will never be hungry again. They will never be thirsty again. The sun will not hurt them. No heat will burn them (see Revelation 7:16).

A crown is waiting for me. I will get that crown for being right with God (see 2 Timothy 4:8).

The city is made of pure gold, as pure as glass (see Revelation 21:21).

The stones of the city have every kind of jewel in them (see Revelation 21:19).

There are many rooms in your Father's house. Jesus is there preparing a place for you (see John 14:2).

There will never be night again. They will not need the light of a lamp or the light of the sun. The Lord God will give them light (see Revelation 22:5).

Only those whose names are written in the Lamb's book of life will enter the city (see Revelation 21:27).

There are so many people that no one can count them. They are from every nation of the earth (see Revelation 7:9).

The angels bow down their faces and worship God (see Revelation 7:11).

They wear white robes and have palm branches in their hands (see Revelation 7:9).

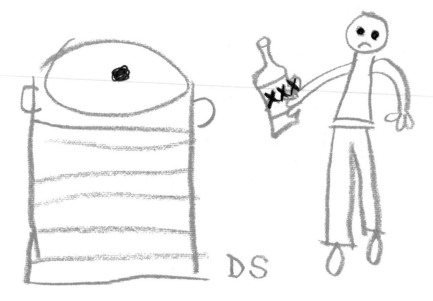

"Why Doesn't He Just Stop?"
LIVING WITH AN ALCOHOLIC

Life with an Alcoholic Parent

The alcoholic parent's needs are considered the most important in the family.

Home is often messy and filled with chaos, disorganization, and confusion.

Discipline is inconsistent. One day the child is scolded for a certain behavior, the next day the same behavior is ignored.

The family rules are unspoken. The rules are: don't talk about family problems, don't express feelings, and don't play.

When the mother is the alcoholic, the children are usually severely neglected. Alcoholism among women is on the increase.

The non-alcoholic parent is often preoccupied with the drinking parent's behavior and therefore is not available to adequately parent the child. Consequently, these children learn that adults are not available to meet their needs.

The children in these homes are praised for their adult-like behavior. However, they are deprived of their childhood.

Each child will respond differently, depending on his or her personality and resources to adapt.

PAT ♡

Dear Heart to Heart,

I am So sad my dad is a alcoholic. I love him so much. I get mad when he brakes promises and maybe if I would be really good he would stop drinking. Please help me!!!!!!

GAINESVILLE, GA 305
PM
6 MAR

Pat-
Gainsville Ga

Mail to
Heart to Heart

Heart to Heart

Dear Pat,

I was so happy to get a letter from you. You wrote so clearly about what is happening at your home, and that helped me understand how it must be for you to have an alcoholic dad. Most kids who have an alcoholic parent say they feel angry and afraid and confused and sad at times. I hope you have friends you can talk to and who will help you. I know that even when kids live with a very diffi-cult problem, they can be happy, and the problem does not have to hurt their lives. You do not have to pretend it's not a problem. It is OK to talk about this to caring people.

It does help to learn to get your needs met by others so you aren't always disappointed with bro-ken promises by the parent who is an alcoholic. There are many kind adults who can be there for you. And best of all, God knows all about what this is like for you and loves you and promises to help you. You can talk to Him anytime. First Peter 5:7 says, "Let Him have all your worries and cares, for He is always thinking about you and watching everything that concerns you."

I prayed for you today, Pat.

Lots of love,

Maria

How Children Feel

Anger, shame, confusion, sadness, and low self-esteem are everyday emotions for a child living with an alcoholic parent.

Children feel responsible for the family problems and believe that something they have done caused them.

Children fear:
♡ not having enough to eat because too much money is spent on alcohol.
♡ riding in a car with a drunk parent.
♡ being abandoned.
♡ being hit when the parents fight.
Children hate parental fighting more than drinking.

They feel embarrassed by the par-ent's behavior.

Children feel sad when they observe one parent covering up for the drinking parent.

They feel frustrated when they are unjustly accused of doing some-thing they were told to do.

Children in alcoholic homes are lonely because they do not receive adequate warmth and nurture.

They feel confused because facts they know to be true are denied.

How Children Adapt

A child may:

♡ assume the responsibilities of a parent by taking care of their brothers and sisters. This is usually the oldest child.

♡ clean house, cook, and take care of the drunk parent. These children become mini-adults.

♡ "go with the flow" and remain flexible, helpful, and adaptive to whatever the circumstance.

♡ demonstrate warm, sensitive behavior because he/she believes that will "fix" the sadness of the alcoholic.

♡ act out in rebellious behavior. These trouble makers learn to "take care of #1."

Children believe they can have some control over their parent's drinking by doing, or not doing, something.

Most children adapt by pretending to outsiders that their parents are nice, normal people.

Children adapt by learning not to feel the pain. They become experts in denial.

Hi, My name is Andrew and I am 10. My dad is a alcoholic. When my dad is drunk he slaps my mom and breaks things. I can't bring a friend over or have fun because my dad might come home. He will not get help and they are getting a divorse. Love, Andr[ew]

Urgent! I AM Scared!

was something you could do to make your dad stop drinking, but that is something only he can decide. You don't need to pretend it's not a problem, and you can get help from understanding grown-ups on how to live with an alcoholic father.

God knows all about what is happening in your family. He loves you and your mom and your dad. You can talk to God anytime and ask Him to help you know what to do. He will always hear you.

Thanks for writing, Andrew. You can write anytime you want. We will always answer.

Much love,

Doris

What to Say

Children remain loyal to abusive parents. If you are angry or disgusted by the parent's behavior you will be dismissed by the child. To be heard you need to give neutral or factual statements about the alcoholic parent.

Children need to know that:

♡ they can be happy even if their parent doesn't stop drinking.

♡ alcoholism is a disease that makes people unable to control their drinking unless they have help.

♡ it's not the "mean boss," nor the flu, nor pressure at home that is causing the problems in the home. It's the disease of alcoholism.

♡ one in six families is touched by an alcoholic. They are not alone.

♡ nothing they have done caused their parent to drink. There is nothing children can do to stop the drinking.

♡ they have the right to tell their own story and be unique in the way they respond.

♡ when children grow up with alcoholics they don't know what normal life is like. They need to know that other parents have stress but they are not alcoholics.

What to Avoid

Don't minimize the stress for children living with an alcoholic parent; i.e., don't tell them just to ignore the parent's behavior.

Don't tell children to count drinks, cover up the drinking, make excuses for the parent's behavior, or hide bottles. They need to stop pretending the drinking isn't a problem.

Don't tell children to take sides when parents fight, or talk back to a drinking parent.

Don't tell children to hide their feelings. It is OK to cry. Say, "Any eight-year-old would cry who had been hurt."

Don't tell children they can't tell others. Some schools have support groups for children living with alcoholic parents.

Don't assume children know when to ask for help. Giving printed information to children about alcoholism teaches the symptoms of the disease.

Don't be afraid to assist with parenting the child of an alcoholic, e.g., affirming their strengths, showing them correct manners, etc.

Don't minimize the risk for children becoming alcoholics at an early age. They may have learned that the way to solve problems is to drink, in addition to having a genetic predisposition to alcoholism.

Pray for my dad so he stops it. He drinks all the time and I am afraid of him. I like your book. Could you write me back.

Yours truly

Dear Heart to Heart,
My mother is an alcoholic. She is gone a lot and sleeps. My grandma tells me to show my feelings but I am afraid. She gave me I KNOW THE Worlds Worst Secret. It helped me understand better.

P.S. Write Back Please!

You're friend,
Annie

Heart to Heart

Dear Annie,

I was SO happy to get a letter from you. You did a very good job of telling how it is for you with your mom's alcoholism. I know it is very hard to live with a parent who abuses alcohol. Many, many children write to us and talk about it. You are not alone!

I'm glad your grandma has told you to talk about your feelings. She is right! It helps make some of the deep sadness and fear go away when others understand how you feel.

I bet you wish there was something you could do to make your mom stop drinking, but that is something only she can decide. You don't need to pretend it's not a problem. You can get help from understanding grown-ups on how to live with an alcoholic parent.

What to Do

Assist children in finding help for themselves whether the parents get help or not.

Include children of alcoholics with your family. They need "borrowed families."

Help them find ways to earn money for sports or school events.

Help them find places to play and have fun away from home.

Tell them what they can do if they feel unsafe at home, e.g., go to the neighbor or call a grandparent.

Give children permission to tell their parents when they are upset by their alcoholic behavior.

Tell children they don't have to explain to friends that they have an alcoholic parent.

Encourage owning a pet if possible. Pets are nonjudgmental friends who give affection in wet licks.

Tell the child that the parent who goes into treatment may substitute Alcoholics Anonymous meetings for the bottle, and may still be unavailable at first.

Preparing for an Emergency

Children need to know alcoholism has serious and progressive physical symptoms.

Help children of alcoholic families develop survival strategies for dealing with the parent's hangovers, frequent accidents, "the shakes," loss of memory, bleeding, or convulsions. Children need help in explaining to friends the physical changes in the parent such as a puffy, reddened face or flabby abdomen.

Tell them, and if necessary show them, how to:

♡ call emergency numbers for fire (if the parent goes to sleep smoking).

♡ call 911 or get help from a near-by adult if there is a medical emergency.

♡ call the police if the parents are fighting and the children are afraid.

♡ carry phone money to call for a ride home if the parent is drunk.

♡ use the bus system so they have alternative transportation if the parent doesn't provide the promised ride.

♡ write things down when a drinking parent makes promises.

♡ call the abused children hot line if they are hit, neglected, or threatened.

Say that any child who lives with an alcoholic parent needs help from an adult. Give them permission to ask for the help they need.

Dear Doris,

How are you? I am fine. Thank you for that book. Now my Dad is going to AA and Mom is going to alanon. I need someone to talk to. I wanted to tell you. What if they start again?

Your Friend,
Gretchen

Dear Doris and Graci,

My Mom said she doesn't drink anymore. But I can't trust her because I found another bottle and I am very sad. I love my Mom but she's hurting herself. I know God loves her. She cusses me and I hate it when she does this. How can I stop her drinking? Please, help me. Write back soon.

Love,
Connie
XOX

Did you know that you are very precious to God? He feels sad when you feel sad. He loves you very much and will help you. I'm sending along some words from the Bible that might help you. Read them out loud and then pick out one or two verses that you like the most and memorize them. Then when you are alone or afraid you can remember what God has said to you through the Bible.

There is nothing you can do to make your mom stop drinking. She will have to choose to stop by herself. But, Connie, you can tell her that it makes you feel afraid when she drinks and that because you love her, you wish she would stop.

Write to us again if you can't find a friend to listen to you. It's important for you to have people who support and encourage you!

Love to you and hugs,

Words of Comfort

"No, I will not abandon you or leave you as orphans in the storm—I will come to you" (John 14:18).

"I am leaving you with a gift—peace of mind and heart! And the peace I give isn't fragile like the peace the world gives. So don't be troubled or afraid" (John 14:27).

"Let him have all your worries and cares, for he is always thinking about you and watching everything that concerns you" (1 Peter 5:7).

"Even when we are too weak to have any faith left, he remains faithful to us and will help us, for he cannot disown us who are part of himself, and he will always carry out his promise to us" (2 Timothy 2:13).

"Just as you trusted Christ to save you, trust him, too, for each day's problems; live in vital union with Him. Let your roots grow down into him and draw up nourishment from him" (Colossians 2:6-7a).

"And I am sure that God who began the good work within you will keep right on helping you grow in his grace until his task within you is finally finished" (Philippians 1:6).

"You are my hiding place from every storm of life; you even keep me from getting into trouble! You surround me with songs of victory. I will instruct you (says the Lord) and guide you along the best pathway for your life; I will advise you and watch your progress" (Psalm 32:7-8).

"So if the Son sets you free, you will indeed be free" (John 8:36).

"Don't be afraid, for I am with you" (Isaiah 43:5).

"May the Lord of peace himself give you his peace no matter what happens" (2 Thessalonians 3:16).

"Nobody Likes Me"
THE CHILD WITH LOW SELF-ESTEEM

Understanding Damaged Self-Esteem

Children's self-esteem can be damaged if:

♡   they feel rejected by their parents. Children will dislike themselves in proportion to the amount of rejection and criticism they experience. They believe the assessment of their parents.

♡   they are not given both love and respect. The two are not synonymous.

♡   they live with a constant diet of degrading words such as "You'll never amount to anything" or "Can't you do anything right?" or "Dummy."

♡   they are pushed beyond their capabilities and consequently experience failure.

♡   they are unfavorably compared with other children.

♡   they are valued for their beauty, money, or possessions. When this happens children have shallow roots on which to base self-esteem.

♡   they believe they are unlikable. Children love others as much as they love themselves. Children who don't like themselves will not invite others to like them.

♡   their school experience is harsh. On many playgrounds name-calling is rampant for the child who in some way is different from other kids. Recess is often a time when children are rejected and their self-esteem undermined.

When we moved To are new house it was hard to because I dont have anybody to play with here and I dont Like ottio and I cry ever night.

weerdo
NERD
DUMMY
stupid
Fatso

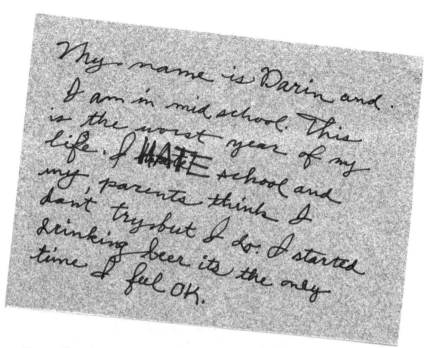

My name is Darin and. I am in mid school. This is the worst year of my life. I ~~HATE~~ school and my parents think I dont try but I do. I started drinking beer its the only time I feel OK.

Dear Darin,

You are really having a hard year at school! Sometimes junior high is really difficult. You said your parents don't think you are trying, but you know you are. Sometimes when kids are having bad feelings about themselves, they have a harder time concentrating on school work. Also, drinking beer makes it harder to study and to do well in school. Is it possible that your parents know that you would be doing better school work if you were not drinking and if you felt better about yourself? Beer does cover up the sad feelings but most kids feel worse about themselves when they are sober again, so it isn't very helpful.

Darin, would you be willing to talk to the school counselor and tell her what you have told me? You deserve to be helped, and you don't have to feel so badly! Thanks for writing. I liked getting a letter from you, and hope you will talk to the school counselor tomorrow.

Much love,

Doris

What to Do

Challenge demeaning self talk, e.g. "I'm so stupid," by saying, "I know you feel badly, but you are not stupid."

Build their confidence:

♡   Ask them their opinion about what to do and then follow their suggestions.

♡   Give them one simple step at a time when you ask them to do something. Children will say they feel dumb because they don't want to fail and prefer not to try.

♡   Teach them to be an expert in something. Success builds self-worth.

Be a friend. Children feel valued when adults say, "I'm your friend. If I can help you, I will."

Spend one-on-one time with each child; this communicates value.

Acknowledge that children who are pretty or bright do have an easier time, but that working hard and having friends are more important abilities.

Help them look for alternatives to solving a problem. Teach them not to give up.

Help children who have weakness in one area to excel in another.

Find other children with similar interests (dance, art, etc.) for them to play with.

Teach them how to fail. Be casual about failures—they are to be expected when learning something new. Set an example by enjoying a game or task even when you don't win.

Teach them how to make and keep friends, e.g., by helping other children, apologizing, sharing, complimenting others.

Encourage playing at activities which are fun, non-competitive, and make children laugh.

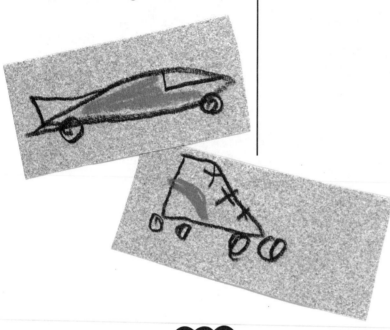

Heart to Heart

Dear Sheila,

It sounds like you are hurting a lot. You said that you need a friend. It does help to have close friends when we feel lonely or sad. One of the best ways to get a friend is to be interested in things others care about and be the kind of person they would like to know. Can you think of someone right now who needs your friendship?

You also mentioned that you believe your parents like your sister more than they like you. I don't know if that is true. Have you asked them about it? My guess is that they may have some different feelings about the two of you because you are different people, but I wouldn't be surprised if they loved you both.

Love,

Dear Loved Jerod,

You must be feeling very, very badly about yourself to think about killing yourself. I am sorry because I know that it must be really hard for you right now. I'm glad that you wrote to talk about it.

You said that kids at school put you down. I'm sure it is hard to ignore their comments. You can be in charge of whether you believe what they say. When kids say unkind things, it is usually because they feel insecure and are trying to make themselves feel superior. People who feel good about themselves don't need to put other people down.

One of the ways that you could protect yourself from their unkind words is to develop friendships with kids who don't put you down, and then avoid or ignore the ones who do.

Jerod, I want to ask you to do something. If you feel like you want to hurt yourself, would you promise me that you will talk to the school counselor before you do anything? I am counting on you to keep your end of the bargain. Please write anytime you feel like it. We like talking with you.

Love,

Doris

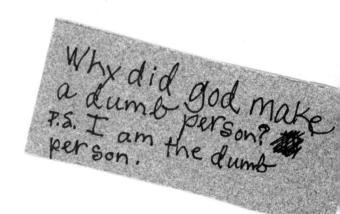

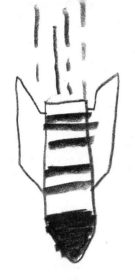

I think I am too old to write you guys a letter because I'm and I know your book Don't Look at Me is for little kids but I just want you to know there is a 12 year old total failure out here. Write please! Sheila

Dear Doris
hi I am in the 9th grade and am thinking about Killing myself but I don't Know how to do it. Kids at school Keep putting me down. I honestly hate myself. How do I find out how to Kill myself? Please write

Jerod

HATE

Dear Doris
Things are going awful. I have to go to the therepist but it never helps me. I would like to have a frend of my own. My parints like my sister best.
Jeremy

Hart to Hart,
I am in the third grade. This
is the second time because I
failed last year and got kept back.
It is embearsing because my
friends are in the forth grade.
Everbody knows.   Danny

Sam Tran
291

LOS ANGELES, CA
P.M.
8 JAN
1991

o: Doris and Graci
S SE AG 181
ran.

Dear Heart to Heart,
My dad calls me stupid
Sam. He even says it in
front of my friends. and
then he laughs. I told
him it wasnt even
funny but he still does it.
Please help me.

Heart to Heart

Dear Danny,

Your handwriting is very nice. Thanks for taking the time and effort to write to us. We think that getting a letter from you is a pretty special thing. It is hard to repeat a grade at school when your friends have gone on to the fourth grade. When I fail at something I wanted to do, I try to just accept what happened and figure out how to make the best of where I am. It will just make you feel badly to think about repeating the grade, so how about thinking about how you can make this year a good one? Ask your mom and dad what you can do to have a good year at school. Ask your teacher what she would suggest you do so you will have a successful year. Start making friends with someone in your classroom.

Danny, everybody has a hard time sooner or later in doing tasks, so it is okay to repeat third grade. Try to think about now and what you can do to have a good year. We think that you will be a major success!

Love from your fan club,

Doris

What to Avoid

Don't lie to children about their abilities. Children's values don't depend on their skill.

Don't minimize the importance of hard work—it always improves ability.

Don't overly protect or encourage dependency.

Don't allow children to blame others for their failures.

Don't assume children will develop good self-esteem without the assistance of an adult.

Don't ignore the value of looking as nice as possible.

Don't imply that everyone else feels good about themselves. Ninety-five percent of adults feel inferior in some way.

Don't expect the child to fill the parent's need to look successful, e.g. excelling in sports or music.

Don't mistake realistic self appraisal with "having a big head."

Don't minimize the value of good self-esteem. It will have an impact on social, spiritual, academic, and emotional well-being.

Don't expect a child to know how to defend himself from taunts without instruction.

Heart to Heart

Dear Manuel,

It is hard to be overweight, and I'm sure that some kids give you a bad time at school about it. That is unkind, and I'm sure it makes you feel very badly. It is pretty hard to make the other kids stop doing that, so I think the best thing to do is to think about what you can do so it won't hurt you so much. Here are a couple of ideas: 1. Spend your time with kids who don't make fun of you and try to avoid kids who do. 2. Ask your PE teacher for some help in losing some weight. Most of us need somebody to be our friend while we are losing weight. It's just too hard to do all by ourselves.

What do you really enjoy doing? Try to become good at doing something you like to do. The more fun you have with nice kids, the less the unkind remarks will bother you.

God loves you. He likes you, too. He is your best friend!

Lots of Love,

Doris

DONNIE

Remember

Once a child adopts a belief about his lack of worth, any damage cannot be "undone" simply by making affirming statements.

Helping children with low self-esteem involves improving their physical appearance, encouraging academic success, and helping them learn how to make friends.

The more specific the praise the more it will be believed.

Affirmation from a broad base of people helps children feel more competent.

Providing focused attention for a short time is more affirming than general attention over a long period of time.

The *quality* of friendships children have is more important than the *number*.

Correction should focus on the behavior, not the child.

Children will believe what they experience before they believe what they hear, but they need to hear love expressed: "I love you." "I like who you are." "You are fun to be with."

Criticism should be given privately, not in front of others.

Dear Mrs. Sanford,
It is hard for me because my folks don't have very much money and I have to wear my big brothers clothes. I feel ugly because I am ugly. I just wish I could buy new stuff.
Well bye.
Trina

WHY did god make me like this

Dear Doris,
I read your book about Patrick and I thought he was like me because I dont have any friends either. The reason nobody likes me is because I am too shy and I dont know what to say to people. Also I ~~have~~ am no good at school and I have zits. Nobody wants to be friends with a person with zits!

I don't know if you ever get a letter from a blind person, but I am. People look at me funny. I can't see them but I know they do anyway.
(P.S. I wrote this for my son)

You are special

See I have written your name on my hand. TRINA Isaiha 49:16

What to Say

Be sure to tell them:

♡ their value doesn't depend on how they feel about themselves.

♡ again and again and in many settings that they have worth.

♡ about your past failures, not just successes.

♡ you believe they will be able to find solutions to their problems.

♡ they have more skill then you in an area. Matter-of-factly refer to the child's strengths in frequent conversation.

Include these statements in your conversations on a regular basis:

♡ "You play the piano so much better than I did at your age."

♡ "I like to watch the way you help Grandma. You are such a kind person."

♡ "I'm so proud to be your parent (friend, etc.). I bet God knew how much I would enjoy being around you."

♡ "I'm so impressed with the way you try so hard."

♡ "I think you made a good decision."

♡ "You get better all the time."

♡ "I admire you."

♡ "Of course your. teacher likes you. Who wouldn't?"

♡ "You are going to be a wonderful dad someday."

♡ "Aren't we lucky to have you in our family?"

How a child is received at the end of the school day will affect his self-esteem, e.g., "Today was your spelling test. I thought about you. How did it go?"

"Nobody Asked Me if it was Okay"
THE DIVORCED FAMILY

Giving the News

All children should be told at the same time.

Children should be told while both parents are still living in the home.

Parents should not give children any false hopes that the marriage problems will be resolved.

Neither parent should blame the other for the divorce.

Tell them the parents have tried to work out the problems; it's not necessary to give personal details.

Explain the confusing issues of divorce: custody, visitations, which house they will live in, division of property as it affects the child.

Tell them that nothing they did caused the divorce to happen and that they cannot "fix" it.

Tell them how often they will see the non-custodial parent after the separation.

Tell the children they are loved by both parents even if they are living with only one parent.

Encourage them to ask questions.

Be prepared to repeat all of the information again and again. Not all reactions will be immediate and each child's response will be unique.

Dear Shana,

Your very special letter came. I am so glad you wrote! Your writing is very nice and easy to read.

I know it is hard when a divorce happens. So much is confusing and sad. Do you tell God how you feel? He really loves you and your mom and dad. You can talk to Him anytime because He promised to always listen, and He will never, never leave you. Some kids think they caused the divorce to happen (but they didn't). And some kids feel mad at God. It is a very scary time.

Shana, God knows all about what has happened in your family, and He loves you more than you can possibly know. God also knows your mommy and daddy hurt inside, too. In the Bible, God's special letter to us, God says, "Don't be afraid, for I am with you" (Isaiah 43:5).

Many children say it helps to ask their mom or dad lots of questions about things they worry about so they can get the real answers. Also, if you tell your mom or dad or other kind adults when you need a hug, that helps.

Honey, even though this is a hard time for you, it _will_ get better.

Lots of love and hugs,

Doris

How Divorce Affects Children

Self-esteem is commonly lowered.

Initially boys seem more affected than girls.

Weekends, vacations, holidays, family weddings all create new stresses.

Friends, neighbors, grandparents often take "sides" and the child loses some of these relationships.

Children believe that if they were "a little older" or "a little younger" it wouldn't hurt so much.

Children measure love by the physical distance between them; i.e., if a parent moves away, he didn't like them.

Children believe they have caused their parents to fight.

DEAr HeArt
It is Not ALways
HAPPy at Are
HOUSE. LOVE
JEFF

How Children Feel

Many children feel rejected by at least one parent.

The trauma for children of divorce can be as severe as trauma over a death, yet they often receive less support when they need it just as much.

Children feel "caught in the middle" between adults at war.

They fear the custodial parent will also abandon them.

Children feel vulnerable and frightened and lonely. Many feel lost and sad.

They worry about the hardships created by lack of money.

Children feel angry because they truly believe the parents could have solved their problems if they had only "tried harder." Divorce is not seen as a solution by children. Even when marriages are unhappy, they wish their parents would stay together.

Children feel embarrassed in front of their friends because of the problems at home.

To: Friend

I need help in my mom & dads divorce. Its still doesnt heel my wounds it teribly hurts my wounds. How can I stop that. I wish I will just forget it today. But never ever stops pleas help me. I cry but crying never helps. I wish I knew what happened and I know I wish it never happend. My mom & dad loved me & the other kids. Why cant they love each other My friends Mom is getting married Boy o, Boy she's lucky. I hope you can teach me how to get that out. thanks

Rachel.

Heart to Heart

Dear Rachel,

You must feel terribly, terribly sad about your mom and dad getting a divorce. One of the hardest things is that you can't do anything to stop it. You said that you wish you knew what happened to cause the divorce. I know that grown-up problems seem pretty confusing. You also said that you wish it had never happened. Honey, I know that is true. I'm glad that you know that they love you and that their problems don't have anything to do with you or their feelings about you.

I wish I could tell you some easy steps that would make your pain go away. I can't. I do know that it helps to talk about your feelings and that it helps to ask the questions you think about. Although it hurts so much right now you don't think you can stand it, most kids eventually feel like they can cope. Divorce in a family happens to many, many children. I bet you know some other kids at school who have families that have had a divorce. Have you talked to them about what helped them feel better?

I am praying for you today, Rachel. You can tell God all about how you feel. He understands and always listens.

Love,

Dorio

How Children Behave

Children sometimes develop physical illness because grief reduces immunity.

Children may misbehave because each parent's rules and discipline are different and what is "right" behavior at one home will be unacceptable in the other.

Boys often have more behavioral problems than girls following divorce.

Children may seek to physically protect a parent from being hurt when parents fight.

Sleeping problems are common.

Fighting often increases with brothers and sisters.

Children have difficulty concentrating, so school performance decreases.

Children manipulate in attempts to get their parents back together.

It is common for children to have bad manners toward adult "intruders" whom the parent dates.

Feeling insecure causes children to be immature, clingy, demanding and to have tantrums and nightmares.

Children may reject parents and withdraw: e.g., "If you don't want me, I don't want you either."

Helping Children Cope

The right technique is not as important as the right relationship. Children sense those who genuinely care about them.

Children will talk about their feelings with adults who spend time with them.

Children are sometimes treated like an adult by the custodial parent. Let children remain children.

Keep a positive attitude. Children can and do heal. They are not "victims of a broken home."

Explain confusing language associated with divorce. Begin by asking, "Do you know what that means?"

Focus on individual children's strengths and what they can do rather than their helplessness in the situation.

It's important to tell children that "Daddy didn't leave you, he left Mommy." (However, children frequently still feel rejection.)

Be cautious about over-optimism, e.g., "Everything will be so much better." Parents are sometimes naive about life after divorce.

Children sometimes choose to talk about their feelings with friends, and this must be accepted.

Allow children the right to mourn their loss.

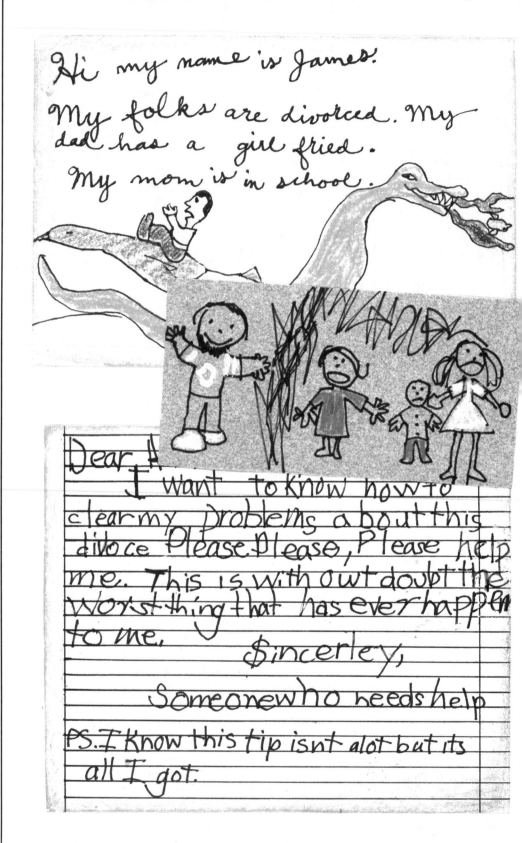

Dear James,

I liked your picture very much and it helped me understand more about what is happening in your family. Your face looks very sad. Your mom and sister look sad, too.

There are so many changes when a divorce happens. You said that your dad has a girlfriend. I wonder how you feel about that? And with your mom at school you might be staying with a babysitter more than you used to. It takes a long time to adjust to the changes. You don't have to be strong and brave. You have been hurt and you have a right to feel sad. Look for things to do that you enjoy doing. Remember that you still have two parents, even if they don't live together. Thanks for writing, James!

Lots of Love,

Doris

Dear Little Friend,

What a courageous one you are to write us! We wish we could be there to hug you and let you talk whenever you need to. Maybe there is an adult teacher or someone at church or an aunt who would be understanding and helpful. There is someone who cares how you feel.

We are so sorry. We know this is the worst thing that has ever happened to you. It must be very hard to have the ones you love the most not loving each other. You won't always feel as badly as you do now, but it will take awhile to feel better.

Remind yourself that you are a very precious little girl and that God knows how you feel and loves you very, very much. Along with our letter are some promises from the Bible. These have been very helpful to us both when we were young and now that we are grandmas.

Let us know how you are doing. By the way, any information we send is free so you didn't need to send the tip. We're sending it back with enough to buy an ice cream cone!

Love and hugs,

Doris

Do's and Don'ts

Do invite children to say what they think and feel, even *bad feelings*.

Don't tell children everything will be "just fine," because for most children this is just not true.

Do say that tears can help wash some of the sadness away and that it is OK to cry.

Don't tell children to be strong or brave.

Do maintain the same rules about chores, bedtime, and homework. It builds security.

Don't be overly indulgent or allow children to control the activities of adults.

Do insist that children sleep in their own beds, not with the parent. Tell them they are safe in their own room—as they have always been.

Do develop a working relationship with the non-custodial parent about issues related to the children.

Don't criticize the other parent in front of the child.

Do adhere rigidly to visiting schedules in the early months.

Don't push children to talk about feelings. Children will decide if and when they want to talk about the divorce.

Do tell children they have a "real family" even if both parents don't live together.

Don't say only good things about the absent parent or the child will wonder why the divorce occurred.

Do read stories about other children whose parents have divorced.

Don't attempt to be both parents to the child.

Do seek out experiences with kid-oriented adults of the non-custodial parent's sex.

I have a hard time with Divorce. I live with my mom, me and my brother. My brother doesn't realy care aboat my Dad But something strange is hapening. I screamed at my Mom two nights in a raw, I want my Daddy. And all of a sudden My aunt sent me a book Please come Home, Please send me some Infomation. Thank-yoy

Margaret

Will I see My Daddy

Dear, Madam I have had some troble choosing on who I should live with, It's hard I cry at night a lot and I cant make-up my mind and I need to talk to someone who will understand MY feelings I read the book called please come home my mom got it for me I'm in 3rd grade I live with my dad My dad has a girlfriend named Lucia and mom has a boyfriend is named Don I like Lucia better than lady. Don. Sincerly, guy Star

By Erica

Heart to Heart

Dear Margaret,

    You must feel very sad and hurt about the divorce. Many times when children are very sad their feelings come out in anger. I bet that is what happened when you yelled at your mom. You probably were just so hurt and missed your daddy so much and all of a sudden it spilled over in anger. Have you told your mom about your feelings?

    I wish so much that I could make all your hurt go away and make everything OK again for you. I can't do that, but I do care about your sadness and will listen anytime you want to write. Nothing you did made the divorce happen. It was a decision that your mommy and daddy made that had nothing to do with you. I know that it is hard to adjust to all the changes that come with a divorce, and I also know that sometimes the grown ups don't know how upset you are.

    You have a very special friend who loves you so much and promises to help you while you are learning to feel better again. This friend is God. He will never, ever leave you and you can talk to Him anytime of the day or night. He is the best friend you can ever have.

    Goodbye for now, Margaret. I am praying for you and I send a giant hug in the mail.

Love,

Doris

Long Term Fall Out

It's a myth that "whatever is good for the parent will be good for the child."

Divorce is not a one time event. Its effects linger.

Children often need three to five years after a divorce to recover their emotional balance.

Children remain faithful to the biological parents, even when a happy remarriage has occurred.

Long term effects for some children include: less independence, more withdrawal, less industriousness, and more unhappiness.

Fear of intimacy, lack of trust, and avoidance of marriage can be long term results for children of divorce.

Children can develop deep inner strength and grow through painful experiences if they are helped to do so.

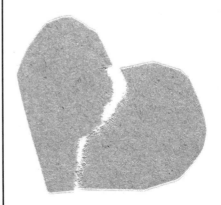

"Why Can't I Tell My Friends?"
LOVING A PERSON WITH AIDS

Teach the Facts

Tell children that there are choices they can make that will limit their exposure to the disease, i.e., they can choose not to take drugs or be sexually active.

Tell children when they are NOT in danger: they can't "catch it" from toilet seats or sneezes or dishes and it's okay to hug and kiss a person with AIDS. A child may be in a classroom with a child with AIDS. The child with AIDS is more in danger than he is.

Tell children when they *are* in danger: they should not use the toothbrush of the person with AIDS or touch their blood or sores.

There is no way to tell if a person has the AIDS virus by looking, so children should practice health safety rules with everyone.

Symptoms such as breathing difficulty, diarrhea, and vomiting should be explained in a matter-of-fact way.

Tell children the disease may cause personality changes and loss of memory.

Explain how the virus can enter the body: body fluids, blood, or by being born to a mom who has it.

Tell the child people all over the world have this disease and that adults and children and babies have it.

Children are sometimes afraid of physical changes in the adult, e.g., pink-brown spots (from Kaposi's sarcoma). Explain they are not bruises and that no one hurt the parent.

This is How You Get AIDS
1 Blood
2 Some body fluids
3 Being born to a mom who has it.

We learned about AIDS at school. I still don't know how you get it. Please tell me. My teacher won't.

I want to know w... Dad used drugs when He knew it wood give him AIDS. Is its too dangerous so WHY did he do it? WHY

TROY

KEITH

Dear Friend,

You asked a very important question: "How does a person get AIDS?" Well, it is almost as important to know how you DON'T get AIDS. You don't get it from hugging, sharing dishes, mosquito bites, water fountains, sneezing, or using the same toilet as a person with AIDS.

You CAN get the virus into your body by getting the blood of a person with AIDS into your blood, by getting body fluids of a person with AIDS into your body, by being born to a mother with AIDS. Just because you have contact with the blood of a person with AIDS doesn't automatically mean that you will get AIDS, only that you could.

The safest thing for a kid to do is not to touch the blood of another person, or pick up syringes from somebody who used drugs in a park, or use a needle for ear piercing that has been used by another person. You never get AIDS by playing with a person with AIDS, or by going to school with a person with AIDS. I'm glad you asked.

Love,

Doris

Dear Troy,

I am so sorry that your dad has AIDS. I know it must be confusing and very frustrating to know that he got it by using drugs. It is very hard to understand why people do things that are dangerous and might give them a disease or cause them to be hurt. Sometimes people don't know that it is dangerous, but you said that your dad *did* know he might get AIDS that way. It must make you feel angry. I'm sure that he is sorry now that he used drugs and got the virus, too.

Maybe it would help you to tell your dad how you feel and how hurt and angry and confused you feel. Talking about your feelings won't fix the problem, but your feelings are very important and you have a right to talk about them. You can also tell other kids to never use drugs! It would probably help you to have an adult who is kind and caring to talk with about your feelings. Can you think of someone you know like this? Thanks for writing to us, Troy. You can write back anytime you want and I will always answer.

Your friend,

General Guidelines

Provide structure and routine whenever possible because there are often extra people coming and going, e.g., nurses, persons checking medical equipment, etc.

Children should learn to wash their hands frequently so the sick adult is not unnecessarily exposed to germs.

Teach children simple tasks which allow them to help, such as making milkshakes, delivering Popsicles.

Persons with AIDS sometimes have tender feet and children need to be careful playing on the bed.

Give children choices whenever you can, e.g., whether they would like to visit the person at the hospital or stay with a sitter.

Keep drugs used to treat symptoms safely out of the reach of children.

Keep in mind that . . .

♡ Since persons with AIDS often live ten years or more, the children may have never known life *apart* from AIDS.

♡ Children may receive mandatory school curriculum about AIDS, but facing the fear, confusion, and grief when someone they love has the disease is another matter.

♡ Children who have first-hand experiences with a person with AIDS will have different attitudes than children with no exposure to the disease.

♡ Children will be more interested in themselves than the person with AIDS. That is part of being a child.

♡ Children usually regress during stress. They may seek comfort that was available to them as a baby.

♡ Children who are "lost in the shuffle" in a home where someone has AIDS may seek the attention they miss by behaving naughtily.

Answering Questions

Remember these guidelines:

♡ tell the truth, no matter what they ask. If you don't know the answer, say so.

♡ don't talk too much. The shortest, true statement is the best one.

Children may ask why people do things that are dangerous which may give them the AIDS virus. Tell them sometimes they don't know it is a dangerous activity at the time.

"How did my parent get AIDS?" can be answered by explaining, "Mommy got it from another person with AIDS" or, "Daddy got it from blood that had the virus in it." If children need to know more, they will ask. (Children also need to know that some people get AIDS because of lack of information about how it is spread.)

If children ask if the parent is gay, ask them what they understand the word to mean. Many children use the word without knowing its meaning.

If children ask, "Did God make my mommy get AIDS?" adults can say

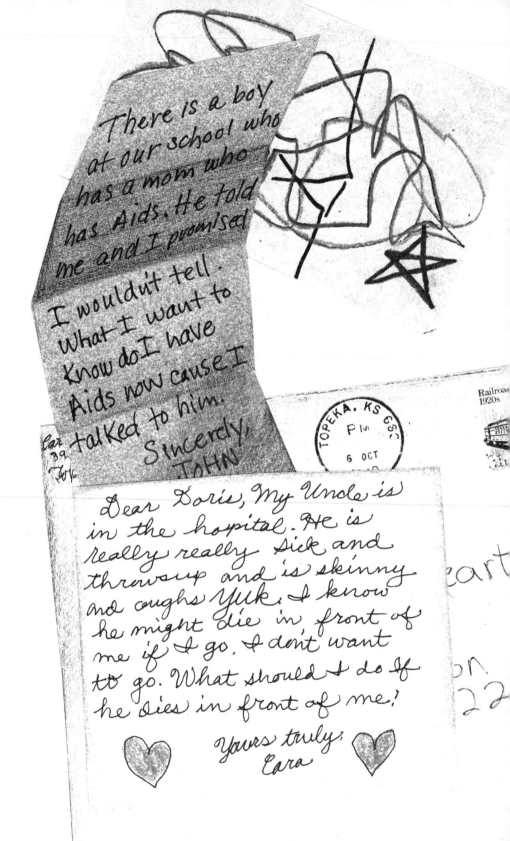

There is a boy at our school who has a mom who has Aids. He told me and I promised I wouldn't tell. What I want to know do I have Aids now cause I talked to him. Sincerely, JOHN

Dear Doris, My Uncle is in the hospital. He is really really sick and throws up and is skinny and coughs Yuk. I know he might die in front of me if I go. I don't want to go. What should I do If he dies in front of me? Yours truly, Cara

Dear John,

Thank you for your letter and for telling me about your friend. I am so sorry that his mother has AIDS. Having a friend who cares is very helpful when you feel badly. He must have trusted you and known that you wouldn't hurt him. I think God has given you a gift of knowing how to be a friend.

You asked if you have the AIDS virus now that you talked to your friend. The answer is that you can't get it by talking with a person. I don't know if your friend has the virus, but even if he did you couldn't get it by talking or playing with him. There are some good children's books that tell about AIDS. Maybe it would help you to read one of them. You can help your friend by listening if he wants to talk about his mom, and by playing with him. Since there isn't any cure for AIDS yet, you can help also by helping him with the sad feelings as his mother gets sicker. You can do that by telling him that it's okay to cry, and by telling him you won't stop being his friend.

Love,

Doris

Dear Cara,

Your uncle sounds very sick. I know it's scary to visit someone who throws up and coughs a lot and is so skinny. I think you are a special girl to go to visit him when it is hard for you, because people with AIDS get very lonely at times.

You said that you are worried that he might die when you are there. That could happen and it is helpful to plan what to do if he does die while you are there, so I'm glad you asked. I think that you are not only caring, but also smart. Usually when a person is getting near death, the adults will know that it is going to happen soon, so you could tell them that if they believe he will die very soon, you would like someone to hold your hand, or explain what is happening, or to leave the room with you. These are all fair requests. Why not tell your parents how you feel now and plan what to do, so you don't have to worry so much. It will still be hard, of course. Any child would feel just like you do. It's okay to be afraid when you don't know what to expect.

Goodbye, dear Cara,

Doris

that God is good and does not make people get diseases.

Teachable moments are selected by the child. AIDS should not be the focus of all discussions.

Reading children's books about AIDS will answer many questions and generate new questions.

Realize that wrong attitudes are more serious than wrong answers to questions about AIDS.

How Children Feel

Children talk about how they feel in the way they behave. Don't push them to talk about their feelings; watch how they act.

Tears are only one language of sadness for children and adults. Some may express their sadness with tears, some may not. Don't push them to cry.

Children's anxieties will escalate as the fears increase of the adult's around them.

Children feel confused by the blaming and condemnation that sometimes accompany the diagnosis.

Children sometimes are not told the name of the disease in order to protect them from possible stigma. Children sense when they have not been told the truth and feel deceived.

Children grieve the loss of friends who will not be allowed to play with them because they live with a person with AIDS. They have a right to grieve this loss and not be overwhelmed by the rage of adults who know how unnecessary this restriction is.

Children frequently feel insecure, guilty, abandoned, sad, and afraid.

Children grieve the repeated separations for hospitalizations which occur as the person becomes sicker. Young children don't have a sense of time about the parent's return home.

A parent with AIDS may be divorced from the custodial parent. The amount of grief these children feel from the death will depend on the amount of bonding they had to that parent.

Children grieve the loss of the other family members who are preoccupied with their own grief.

They feel angry, which may be the result of helplessness, fear, and grief.

Helping Families Cope

Children need stability and long term caregivers. Children of single parents need opportunities to emotionally attach to the adults who will care for them after their parent's death.

Parents with AIDS sometimes emotionally detach because they are so sick. They don't always have the energy to address the needs of the children. When this occurs other adults can support the children.

Comfort needs to be addressed toward what *children* fear, not what the adults fear: e.g., children may fear the IV equipment more than the germs.

Me and my brother go to play therapy since our Dad died. I a 9 years old. All the other kids here had their Mom or Dad died of AiDs. We were wondring if our Dad went to heaven.
David
PS write back

My dad and Gary want me to come over anytime I want but Gary has AIDS and my grandma won't let me xcept when she takes me. Won't my dad get it?

My best friends Dad says people who get AIDS deserve to die but I like that boy Washington in your book where he helped his friend with AIDS. Love, Janice

Dear David,

I am glad that you and your brother go to play therapy and can talk with other children who have had a mom or dad die from AIDS. It is hard to think that nobody understands how you feel, and I bet it helps to be with other kids who know a lot about how you feel.

You asked a very important question: Did your dad go to heaven?

The Bible, which is God's book, says, "Your Father in heaven is not willing that any should perish" (Matthew 18:14). He wants everyone to be able to come and live with Him in heaven forever. But God's book also tells us there is one thing that can keep us from coming to live with Him, and that is sin (Romans 3:23). We have all done things which do not please God. God is perfect and cannot live with any sin in heaven, so He made a way for our sin to be taken away. "For God so loved the world that he gave his one and only son (that's Jesus) that whoever believes in him shall not perish but have eternal life" (John 3:16). Jesus took the punishment for all of our sins. If we want to live in heaven after we die, we need to believe these things and invite Jesus into our lives and ask him to forgive our sins.

In John 1:12 the Bible says, "To all who received Him, He gave the right to become the children of God." Then our names are written in a special book in heaven (Revelation 21:27). So, David, that is how a person can know if he is going to heaven. Since every person must do this for himself, I don't know if your dad asked Jesus into his heart. His going to heaven doesn't have anything to do with having AIDS.

Love,

Doris

Dear Janice,

You wrote a great letter! I feel sad when I hear people say that someone with AIDS deserves to die, and I'm *so* glad that there are lots of loving people like you out there who want to be like the little boy in the story we wrote. When we care and want to help we make it easier for the people who are sick with this disease, and we are acting like God wants us to act. So you are God's kind of girl! I like who you are!

Lots of Love,

Be sensitive to disappointments which occur because daily life frequently depends on schedules of the ill person.

Although children may not initially grieve the death of the non-custodial parent, grief may surface years later for the relationship they never had. They'll need support whenever the grief emerges.

Grandparents, often a source of comfort for their grandchildren, may be enraged at the diagnosis of AIDS and/ or preoccupied with their own grief and be unable to focus on the children's needs. When this happens, children will need other sources of comfort.

Children may learn for the first time about the parent's homosexuality at the time of the diagnosis of AIDS. For the older child, this will bring additional questions.

Adults need to be transparent and vulnerable about their feelings. Children hear more than is intentionally told them or taught, and they have built in lie detectors when they are deceived.

Support children's needs to run, make noise, and have friends over to play. Provide "time out" from the sickness of AIDS and from being quiet and good.

Children need to feel helpful. They can contribute their art work and decorations for the sick person's room.

Dear Heart to Heart,
It dosnt seem fair.
My dad has AIDS from
blood when he was
sick. Why das this
happen to me. My
dad will die. I am
afraid.

My momy and daddy
always figting and
they dont live togeth
I so sad and lonesome.
My dad said he would
take me fishing but
he never did.
                    Jackson
PS My dad has a
disees but I dont know
what

I heard about babies
who have AIDS and it
makes me pretty sad.
Why don't they give them
medacen and make them
better? OR DO A
          OPERA SHUN
How come God makes
babies get AIDS? Just
~~answer~~ write back if you
know the answer.
                Dannielle

Dear Dannielle,

You wrote such a wonderful letter and asked great questions! I know you said I didn't need to write back unless I know the answers to your questions, but I wanted to write and talk about your questions even if I don't know all the answers.

Dannielle, some of the hard questions will only be answered after we get to heaven and can ask God. One of the very hardest things of all is having to wait to find out the reasons certain things happen, but I don't want to tell you any lies. Adults just don't know all the answers.

You asked why the doctors don't have medicine or an operation that will make babies with AIDS get better. The answer is that so far there isn't any medicine that will cure AIDS, and an operation wouldn't cure it either. There are medicines that help people with AIDS live longer and feel better.

You also wanted to know why God "makes babies get AIDS." This is a question that many grown-ups also ask. I know part of the answer, and the rest will have to wait until we get to heaven. God doesn't make babies get AIDS. Babies and children and adults all get AIDS from a virus that gets in their bodies in certain ways. Sometimes people get the virus by doing dangerous activities, but babies only get it because their bodies were exposed to the virus. The babies couldn't do anything to prevent getting it. We know that God allows people to make choices, even when it will hurt them. The Bible says that when we are in heaven nobody will have AIDS, or any other diseases.

Keep asking questions, and tell God how you are feeling. I feel sad about the babies who die from AIDS, too.

Lots of Love,

Doris

"Why Does She Do That?"
WHEN A GRANDPARENT IS DEMENTED

Teaching Children about Dementia

Have a family meeting and tell children the exact name of the illness and review the symptoms, e.g., angry outbursts and not remembering grandchildren's names. Also develop a plan for helping the grandparent.

Tell children:

♡ the kitchen is a dangerous place for a grandparent with dementia, therefore poisons such as bleach and furniture polish are locked up in order to protect the grandparent.

♡ the grandparent could wander and get lost.

♡ the grandparent's behavior may change in a few months or not for years, but there is no cure for most dementing illness.

♡ there is no shame in having a grandparent with dementia. It can happen to anyone.

♡ they didn't cause the disease and it is no one's fault.

Teach children that they can be important helpers and that they are appreciated.

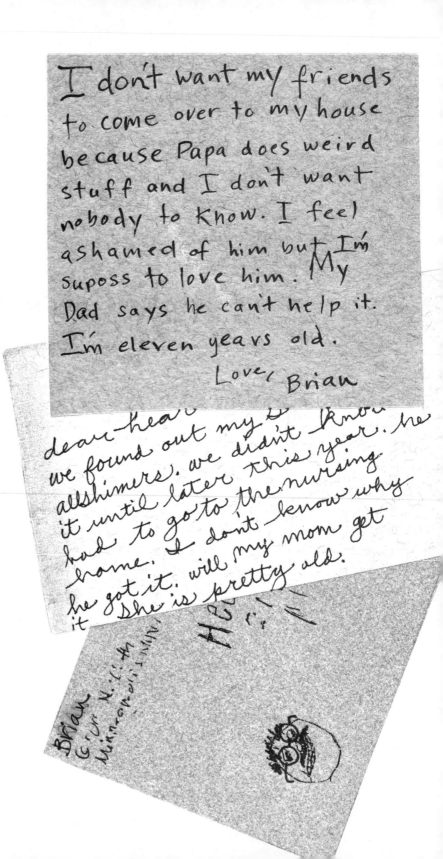

I don't want my friends to come over to my house because Papa does weird stuff and I don't want nobody to know. I feel ashamed of him but I'm suposs to love him. My Dad says he can't help it. I'm eleven years old.

Love, Brian

dear hea... we found out my ... allshimers. we didn't know it until later this year. he had to go to the nursing home. I don't know why he got it. will my mom get it ... she is pretty old.

Brian
G'... N. ...th
Minneapolis, Minn...

Heart to Heart

Dear Brian,

I can understand that it is hard for you to have friends over to your house to play when you don't know for sure what your grandfather will do. I think you are feeling the way many children feel who have a grandparent with dementia. Your dad is right in saying that Papa can't help what he is doing.

We need to think of ways for you to get some help since your grandfather won't change. One suggestion is that you could share a children's book about Alzheimer's with one of your friends and explain why your Papa has done what he does. Other children can understand if they are told about it. It is nobody's fault that your Papa has dementia so you really don't have to feel ashamed. It is just a sad thing that happened. Thanks for writing, Brian.

Love,

Doris

Questions and Answers

"What is the matter with Grandma?"

She has a brain disease called Alzheimer's which makes her sometimes get mixed up or forget or not want to play with you.

"What caused it?"

We don't know and at this time there is no cure.

"Will I get it when I'm older?"

Probably not. Most older people don't.

"What will happen to her?"

Usually people are sick with the disease for about ten years, they get worse and finally they die.

"When will Grandma get worse?"

We don't know. Some grandparents are okay for five years.

"Does it hurt?"

Grandma feels sad about the changes, but she doesn't hurt at all.

"Why does Grandma have to go to a nursing home?"

I can't take care of her at home as well as she will be cared for there. She will like the routine and feel safe.

How Children Feel

How children feel will depend on the relationship they have with their grandparents, and the amount of change that the illness brings to the children's life.

Children mourn the loss of a special friend and companion as the grandparent loses interest in them and their activities.

Children may also feel the loss of the parents because of their preoccupation with the demented grandparent.

Ultimately the grandparent will die, and the child will experience grief.

Children may be anxious, confused, and hurt. They wonder why an adult is less responsible than a child.

Children feel embarrassed by the grandparent's behavior in front of their friends.

They feel sad when they receive the displaced anger of their exhausted parents.

Children dread mealtimes because someone is often upset by the grandparent's behavior.

They may resent the time necessary to care for the grandparent and the loss of the flexibility in the parents' schedule for their own activities.

Children often are expected to help with duties normally assumed by the parent, and they resent this.

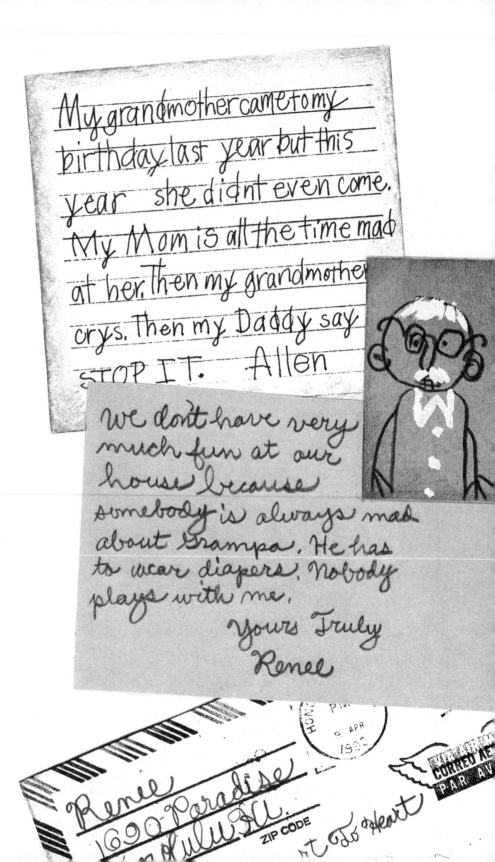

My grandmother came to my birthday last year but this year she didnt even come. My Mom is all the time mad at her. Then my grandmother crys. Then my Daddy say STOP IT.   Allen

We don't have very much fun at our house because somebody is always mad about Grampa. He has to wear diapers. Nobody plays with me.
Yours Truly
Renee

Heart to Heart

Dear Allen,

It sounds like there is sometimes a lot of difficulty at your house because of your grandmother's problems. I know it changes your life at home to have these difficulties. It must make you feel badly to have your mom and dad upset and your grandmother crying.

God knows all about how it is at your house and how you feel. He cares about your grandmother, too. One thing that might help you is to ask your parents what has changed your grandmother's behavior so you will know why she didn't come to your birthday party. Also, it might help you to tell your parents how you feel about the anger and crying. I know you are sad and I wish I could make it easier for you.

Love,

Doris

Heart to Heart

Dear Renee,

It sounds like the adults at your house are pretty busy with taking care of your grandpa and that you don't get as much attention as you would like. That must be very hard for you. Would it help to ask your parents if you can have a friend over to play with you, or go to visit a friend? It must seem confusing to have your grandpa wear diapers. I'm glad that you read our book about Alzheimer's and know that all these changes are caused by a disease. You are an important helper, but you also need time to play and have fun. I'm glad that you told me how you feel.

Your friend,

Doris

Helping Children Cope

Help children laugh about humorous behavior in the grandparent.

Children will always feel the stress of the parents. As care-giving demands increase, take children out for play experiences and to have fun.

Answer questions honestly and immediately.

Allow children to choose the level of involvement in helping.

Allow children whatever feelings they have. Don't expect them to be attached to a grandparent they have never known or one they never knew before the dementia.

Children can share what they have learned about dementia at school. This gives them an opportunity to be "expert" in something that other children don't know. It also provides a platform for them to explain their grandparent's behavior.

Help find resources for information and support, e.g., books for children about the disease.

Realize that solutions that worked well for the children in one family will not be appropriate for another.

Ways Children Can Help

Walking with the grandparent in enclosed areas.

Dancing, singing, or playing music for the grandparent.

Turning the pages on a daily calendar.

Giving the grandparent fresh fruit each day.

Helping maintain a structured routine by assisting with brushing teeth and making the bed.

Decorating the grandparent's room with drawings and flowers.

Returning the grandparent's possessions to the same place each time: glasses, dentures, money.

Telling the grandparent they like to help him and that they love him.

Reminding the grandparent about the season, time of day, and address.

Checking to see that the grandparent is safe when he wanders from the room.

My name is Natasha. My Grandma lives with us but she doesn't act like a real Grandma. She just sits in her chair or follows Mama all around. I wish she liked me again.

I read your book about Marias Gramma gets mixed Up. My Gramma gets lost so we have to take her for walks. she doesn't Know where our house is at, I had to give her my bedroom when she moved in
Sarah

MATThew 9

Dear Natasha,

It must make you very sad to watch your grandma withdraw from you and change from being the grandma she used to be. Sometimes older people have a disease that makes them lose interest in what is happening. I think that may be what has happened to your grandma. It isn't that she chooses not to play and respond to you, but it is because of the disease that she acts the way she does. You have every reason to feel sad. Your grandma needs your help now and you can make a big difference in her life by talking to her and helping her. It would be a special gift.

Lots of love,

Doris

Dear Sarah,

I think the grandma in our story, <u>Maria's Grandma Gets Mixed Up</u> must be like your grandma in some ways. Does your grandma have Alzheimer's? I'm glad that you take your grandma for walks, so she doesn't get lost. You said that you had to give up your bedroom when she moved to your house. Thank you for doing that, Sarah. It is a big help to your grandma to have a special granddaughter who helps.

Love,

Doris

Effects on the Family

Families often don't know the cause of the changes in the grandparent for several years. The stress they feel has accumulated over this period.

As the disease progresses, anxiety and the demand on family members increase.

Decisions about care givers and nursing home placement cause stress.

Because many dementing illnesses last seven to ten years, some families consider them a "slow funeral."

The grandparent's impaired judgment, limited communication, and personality changes can spoil family holidays.

If the grandparent lives at home, there is often less sleep for the care givers.

Family member self-esteem decreases as frustration, shadowing, irritability, and apathy in the grandparent increase.

Many families feel guilty when the grandparent is placed in a nursing home.

Family members are sometimes verbally abused by the grandparent with dementia.

The family is often "burned out," lonely, and financially devastated.

They may feel angry, confused, overwhelmed, afraid, and depressed.

Jerome

"For Your Own Good"
LIVING IN FOSTER CARE

How Children Respond

Children respond to the loss of their family with grief just as they would to any other major loss.

Children's reactions will not be the same as those of the adults. Children don't perceive placement to be "protective" nor "for their own good."

Children feel they have done something wrong and that's why they are in a foster home.

Children's responses are influenced by:

♡ their sense of self-worth prior to placement.

♡ the circumstances of their removal from the parent's home. Some have little warning while they watch their parents being arrested.

♡ the type of lifestyle they are used to. The foster home may be very different, e.g., eating vegetables, doing homework, going to church.

♡ their belief about *why* the foster parents are taking care of them.

♡ the difference in the type of discipline they are used to.

Children initially "honeymoon" in the early weeks or months.

They are on their best behavior while they check things out.

After the "honeymoon," children must test the "What will happen if" possibilities.

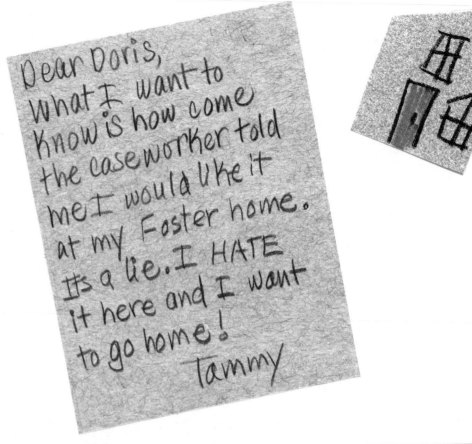

Dear Doris,
What I want to know is how come the caseworker told me I would like it at my Foster home. Its a lie. I HATE it here and I want to go home!
Tammy

KIMMY

Dear Tammy,

It is hard to go to a foster home and I'm sure that it must be very different from what you are used to at your parents' home. You said the case worker told you that you would like it, but that you actually hate it. Lots of children feel that way when they have to adjust to such a different environment and rules. It takes time to feel secure.

I bet you feel sad about having to be separated from your parents, too. Sometimes when kids feel very, very sad the feelings come out as mad feelings. You have a right to feel sad, honey. You didn't do anything bad to make you go into foster care. What happened was not your fault. When hard things happen one thing you can do is to try to adjust to the new situation and not fight it. See if there are new things you can learn there. It won't make all the hurt go away, and it doesn't mean that you will like being in foster care, but it will make it a little easier for you. You can write any time you want, Tammy. I'll always answer.

Your friends,

Doris

WHAT I LiKe about Living here: nothing
WHAT I HATE about Living here: everything

Dear Heart to Heart ♡ ♡
When I was with my REAL mom I could eat what I wanted. Now I have to eat rotten stinken awful vegtables. I am hungry all the time but not for this kind of food,

Helping Children Cope

Let children know about anticipated changes.

Encourage children to put their feelings into words.

Tell children they aren't to blame for their parents' problems or for their placement into foster care.

Tell children what they can do so they don't have to wonder.

Together with the child maintain a journal with pictures of friends, school, and foster family, plus accomplishments.

Don't make promises that you cannot keep.

Allow children to have personal possessions that they don't have to share.

Use logical consequences in disciplining.

Don't make mountains out of mole hills. Some things are not worth addressing initially.

Most foster children have difficulty with school work. Helping them succeed with school work is valuable.

Nights are especially scary. Having a routine, reading a story, and giving hugs help.

Children try to fill up emotional emptiness with food. Provide access to low sugar snacks.

Adjusting to Two Sets of Parents

Many natural parents of foster children simply don't know how to parent, nor do they have any understanding of normal growth and development.

Children feel protective of their natural parents. To criticize them is to be alienated from the child.

Children may have simplistic solutions to their parents' problems, e.g.,"My mom can stop getting drunk and I will go home."

Children develop fantasies about their natural parents. The less they see them, the more the fantasy grows. Be gentle in challenging the child's glowing description of his parents by saying, "I know you wish that were true."

Children lie about past or future experiences in order to gain self worth.

Children are frequently upset by visits with natural parents.

Children may attempt to play foster parents against natural parents.

Foster parents may feel critical of natural parents and natural parents may feel critical of foster parents. Neither have all the truth.

If children must choose between known and emotionally unhealthy parents, and unknown but emotionally healthy parents, they will always pick the known.

My Dad had a lot of money and he bought me lots of presents and I had a new bike. Now I have nothing. Do you get it why I don't like this foster home?
Rian

what made me madest is:
① They didn't give me all my clothes back.
② my mom broke the wooden spoon on me
③ I go to my mom then I go to a foster home the I go to my mom's again

To: DORIS AND GRACI
I have Bad dreams and I cry at night Sherry tells me to SHUT UP but I cant. I don't like living in this foster home.

I should be with my gramma.

Heart to Heart

Dear Rian,

I'm glad you wrote. A letter is a special gift because it took you time to write about your feelings and I am so glad that you sent the letter! You said that your dad gave you gifts and that he had lots of money and that now you don't have all those things at the foster home.

Dear Rian, I want to tell you about something strange that sometimes happens to kids when they get into foster care. Maybe this is what has happened to you? Here it is: sometimes when kids haven't seen their parents for awhile, they forget all the bad stuff that happened and the good things become even better than they actually, honestly, really were. It isn't that kids lie about it, it's just that it gets mixed up about what really happened and what they pretended happened. I don't know if this is true for you, but you might want to think about it and let me know. I'm glad you wrote to us.

Love,

Doris

Building Self-Esteem

Speak only for yourself and don't speak for the natural parent; i.e., say, "I love you" but don't say, "Your mother loves you."

Talk at eye level with children when you praise them.

Give affection freely. Smiling, pats on the back, or extra gentleness in helping children affirm them.

Tell children specifically what you like about their behavior or project.

Have visual displays of successes, e.g., graphs with stickers for jobs accomplished.

Celebrate victories with a party.

One to one time will leave children feeling special, even if it is ten minutes to read a story.

Allow children to make choices whenever they can.

Sit beside children while they do their homework—this makes them feel supported.

Give children opportunities to explore new skills, e.g., build something.

Enhance their appearance by good grooming and dressing.

Don't let children hurt themselves or others.

Teaching Children What to Say

It is helpful to imagine potential questions and role play an imaginary conversation when teaching children how to talk about themselves.

The most common questions are:

♡ What is your name? (The child should give his legal name, not his foster name).

♡ Where did you come from? (The child can state the city).

♡ Why are you in a foster home? (The child can say, "I'm staying here for a while because my folks have problems.")

The child's responses should be truthful, but brief. Caution children about saying too much about their past. This will protect their self-esteem.

Encourage them to talk about their strengths, not their problems, when meeting strangers.

Tell them not all people are entitled to detailed answers to their questions. If invasive questions are asked, the child can say, "That's family information." Children need help in identifying who they can talk with about their past. They can be taught to ask the same questions of the person who is asking them questions.

I am real sorry that I told my teacher about my Dad did bad things to me. I dont want to tell you what. My teacher the police and they made me come here. nothing bad happened to my Dad everything bad happened to me.

Sincerely,
Jennifer

Dear Doris,
I feel sad and mad when my Mom says she will come and see me and she never does. How can I get to make her come. I get to go home when she stops using drugs.
Laurie

Dear Jennifer,

I am so proud of you for doing the right thing, even though it was very hard for you to do. It was the only way to make the bad things stop that your Daddy was doing to you. I think it must be very hard for you to feel that because you told, you were hurt again. But dear precious Jennifer, if you hadn't told your teacher, the abuse would happen again and again and again. Your teacher was required to tell the police.

Your daddy can choose to get help for his problem so he won't do it to any other girl. You are not being punished for telling by being sent to a foster home. You did the brave, right thing. I wish your dad hadn't hurt you because you deserve to be treated like a loved, priceless, special girl. God knows all about this and promises to be with you every day while you are at the foster home.

Lots of love and hugs,

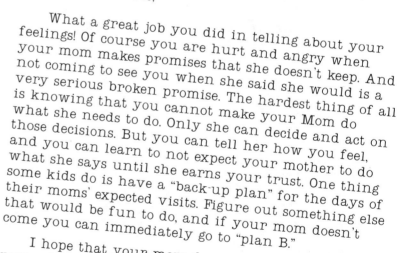

Dear sweet Laurie,

What a great job you did in telling about your feelings! Of course you are hurt and angry when your mom makes promises that she doesn't keep. And not coming to see you when she said she would is a very serious broken promise. The hardest thing of all is knowing that you cannot make your Mom do what she needs to do. Only she can decide and act on those decisions. But you can tell her how you feel, and you can learn to not expect your mother to do what she says until she earns your trust. One thing some kids do is have a "back-up plan" for the days of their moms' expected visits. Figure out something else that would be fun to do, and if your mom doesn't come you can immediately go to "plan B."

I hope that your mom does stop using drugs—but remember, that is not a choice you can make for her. She will have to choose to do it for herself. I am going to pray that your mom will stop using drugs. You deserve the care and love of your mother. While you wait for her to get treatment, I hope there are other loving adults who can help you.

Love,

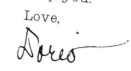

I don't like when people ask me how come my parents didnt want me. They just had problems.

Troy

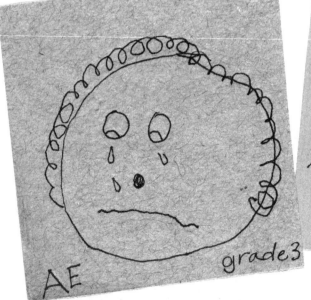

I had to come to a foster home cause my mom and my Dad got busted by the cops for selling drugs. They are in jail I get to visit on Tuesdays. I cried and screamed when the police put hand cuf on them. Please wright.

Wayne

My foster dad is nice but my foster mother is real mean. The other kids that live here brake my toys and steal things. How can I make them stop doing it.

AE   grade 3

Heart to Heart

Dear Wayne,

I felt so sad about what happened to you. It must have been very, very hard to watch your parents being arrested for selling drugs. Even when kids know that what their parents are doing is wrong, it still hurts to see them go to jail. You must have felt scared and hurt and angry. Any child would.

You really didn't have any warning that you would be coming to live at a foster home and didn't have time to get ready to move. That makes it especially hard. I'm sorry your parents made some wrong choices, but I know that you can decide for yourself what you will do about drugs and other important decisions. I bet you will decide *not* to have anything to do with drugs! It is OK to tell your parents that you are hurt by what they did. We wish we could make everything just right for you, Wayne, because you deserve that. We can't fix it, but we do send you lots of love and want you to know that we are your friends.

Love,

Doris

My Foster parents are very good to me and I am lucky to live here. They are going to adopt me when they can!

Traits of Healthy Families

Children are usually placed in foster care because they come from families with inadequate parenting. Children can return to their natural parents as they learn and practice the characteristics of a family:

Healthy parents are in it "for the long haul"—they don't run away from hard times.

The parents refuse to feel rejected. They know that the child who rejects them is hurting. They are stubborn in their acceptance of their children.

The parents get involved in the details of the children's life.

They expect obedience and appropriate behavior from children. They don't ignore bad behavior.

They have realistic goals for each child and honor progress.

Healthy parents say, "I love you," and "You were right and I was wrong."

They don't expect nor want all the children to be alike.

They defend each other from outside criticism.

They value the child's feelings and opinions even when they are different from the parents'.

They laugh easily and often.

They have a belief system that gives meaning to hard times.

They know how to play and have fun without spending money.

Family members can say how they feel and know they will be accepted.

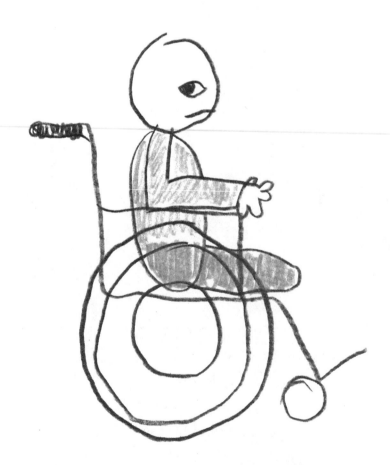

"Will the Cancer Make Me Die?"
EXPERIENCING A LIFE-THREATENING ILLNESS

Talking about Cancer

Children are usually far ahead of adults in readiness to talk about the possibility of death.

Children listen not only to what is said, but what is not said. Avoiding the subject of what will happen "must mean that it is really bad or they would tell me."

If children are not talking about their fear of dying they may be sensing that the parents are unable to talk.

Children of five or six years are old enough to know that they might die from the disease.

Balance truth with hope by answering only the questions the child asks.

Truth is more supportive than deception. Don't tell the terminally ill that they will get better. Say that you will stay with them and that the medicine will help take away the pain.

Invite questions by asking, "What do you wonder about?"

Timing is everything. The questions a child has one time will not be the same questions at another time.

Focus on immediate joys rather than long range fears.

Be simple and concrete with explanations. Compare each experience to something the child knows.

Children can't tolerate long discussions about sad things. They need to distract themselves with play.

Children can be told that the act of dying doesn't physically hurt.

I AM DARIN. THE THINGS I HATE MOST ABOUT HAVING LEUKEMIA:
1 THROWING UP FROM MEDICINE
2 IVS
3 BONE MAROWS
4 BEING BY MYSELF
WOULD YOU WRITE ME A STORY ABOUT ANOTHER KID WHO HAS LEUKEMIA. MAKE IT HAVE A HAPPY ENDING.

The nurse said she wouldn't do my IV til my Mom got back but she did. Can she do that? Another thing I am going to have a bone marrow transplant and my brothers going to do it to me. After that I won't have leukemea anymore.

Heart to Heart

Dear Darin,

Wow! It sounds like you have been pretty sick and that you have had medicine, IVs, bone marrow tests, and that sometimes you have had to be separated from your family. Those are all hard things.

You asked us to write a story about another kid with leukemia and make it have a happy ending. You know, Darin, I want to tell you something that may be hard to understand. Please write me again if you want to talk more about it. What I want to tell you is that we each write our own story and we can make our story have a happy ending. It doesn't depend on circumstances. Even when we have sad or hard things happen to us, we can choose how we will respond to those things. You don't have to pretend that you like IVs and bone marrows, but you can learn to think about other things more and more, and learn to enjoy the good things that are in your life. It doesn't make the bad go away, but it does make it easier to tolerate. So, you are writing your life story now and I think you can make it have a good ending.

I liked the way you could tell the truth about what you like and don't like!

Goodbye, special friend!

Doris

ZAP

Understanding Feelings

For hospitalized young children nothing is more frightening than being separated from parents.

Children who are six to nine years old are more afraid of painful procedures, such as bone marrow tests, than of the illness itself.

Young children don't know the difference between minor and life threatening symptoms, so their emotional responses may be inconsistent with the seriousness of the problem.

Children deal with fears by regressing to earlier "baby-like" behavior. Comfort the child according to his behavior, not age.

Children don't always talk about their feelings. Adults can express the unstated feelings of the child, "I know you are frightened. I will help you."

A child's crying may be more out of confusion, fear, and separation than pain.

A child's previous experience with hospitalization will affect what is frightening. Children generalize from the past.

How children emotionally respond to life-threatening illness will be affected by other demands in his life, e.g., a new baby in the family, entering school, etc.

Nothing is more frightening for parents than fear for the life of their children. Children feel that anxiety; they have built-in lie detectors. Don't lie about your feelings. It is OK to admit to children you feel sad or worried.

Effects on Siblings

Parents have known life apart from the child who may die but a sibling may not. Grief may be devastating.

The illness of a sibling removes the security that parents can protect them from all harm.

They may be over-protected by the parents.

If the family has trouble talking about cancer, the children must deal with their feelings alone.

A sibling may have been a bone marrow donor. If the transplant failed, he may feel HE failed.

The particular relationship of the child to the one who is sick will have an impact on the adjustment. The closer they are, the harder the grief.

Children who did not get along well sometimes feel a need to be "punished" when a sibling is ill.

Children may feel that the parents are upset about the sick child because they are not satisfied with the other children.

Siblings are often expected to be more independent, more mature, more self-sufficient at a time when they are most under stress.

My little brother is a jerk and he thinks because he has a problem with his heart that everybody has to do what he says. What about me? Don't I count? NIKKI

What I hate about cancer is that everybody thinks my brother is famace or something. He gets all the presents and I get all the NOTHING! Mikie

Ever since my sister got cancer my Dad is mad all the time and won't let me go to the park to ride my skateboard. Tell him to quit being mean to me. It's not my fault.

Heart to Heart

Dear Nikki,

It is very hard when you have a brother with a heart problem who gets so much extra attention. Lots of kids tell us that they don't like it when that happens. Sometimes parents get so worried that they give more attention for awhile to the child who is sick. It is okay for you to feel jealous. Any child would feel that way. And it is good to say out loud what you are feeling. Have you told your parents that you want more attention right now and that you are angry about your brother telling you what to do? It might also help to know that your little brother doesn't want to be sick and that he might be acting badly right now because he is scared. Some kids do that. I'm glad that you wrote to us. We're your friends.

Love,

Doris

Helping Siblings

Bring diversional games while they are visiting at the hospital.

Give them art projects to help express their feelings.

Give them focused, affirming attention. Parents tend to idolize a child with cancer and expect too much of the other children.

Keep life as normal as possible for them. Help with transportation to school events, play with friends, etc.

Assist them in useful projects, e.g., making cookies for families at the hospital. Siblings feel helpless.

Give them permission to have fun and "forget" about their sick brother or sister.

Tell brothers and sisters that nothing they did caused the illness.

Allow them to help with the care if they choose.

Look for a support group for them.

What to Avoid

Don't give a child time tables for treatments of the disease.

Don't minimize the ability of the child to cope. Many children are beautiful examples of courage.

Don't tell the parents you know how they feel, even if you have had a child with cancer.

Don't tolerate behavior in the child which would not have been acceptable before the illness.

Don't hide the deaths of other children at the hospital.

Don't promise that the child won't die and that the medicines will make him/her "better."

Don't push suggestions on the parents. The way they are handling this is the right way for them.

Don't criticize the doctor. Parents who trust the doctor will handle the child's illness better.

Don't be afraid to seek a second medical opinion.

Don't be afraid to refuse visitors. Chemotherapy reduces the child's immunity.

Don't lie about pain. If it will hurt, say so and then distract the child.

Don't expect much emotion when the child is told about the cancer. Children don't know what this means.

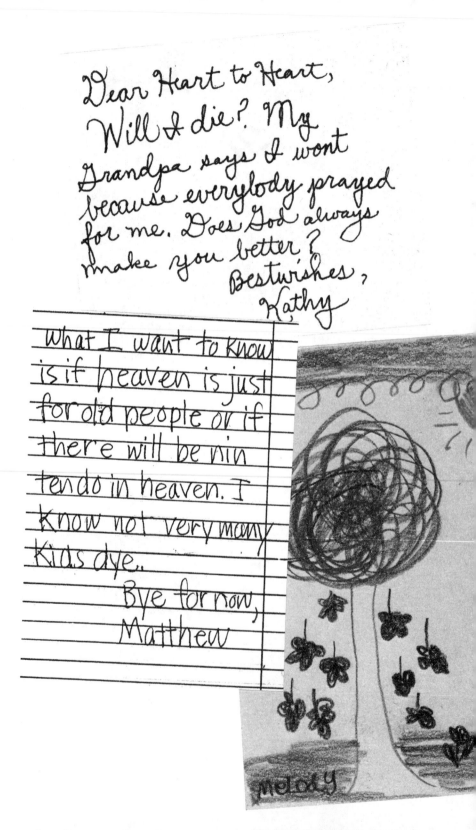

Dear Heart to Heart,
Will I die? My Grandpa says I wont because everybody prayed for me. Does God always make you better?
Best wishes,
Kathy

What I want to know is if heaven is just for old people or if there will be nintendo in heaven. I know not very many kids dye..
Bye for now,
Matthew

melody

Heart to Heart

Dear Matthew,

You asked about heaven and if there will be video games there for kids to play with, or if heaven is just for old people. There are so many questions about heaven and what it will be like. Most of it will be a big surprise, but there are some things that God has told us in the Bible about heaven. One of these facts is that God says nobody in heaven ever cries or is sad (that verse is in Revelation 7:17), so that means everybody in heaven is happy. Since lots of children have died there must be things far beyond your wildest imagination to make kids happy in heaven. Don't you wonder what will be there? It sounds to me like it will be better than video games, even! What a great question you asked!

Hugs,
Doris

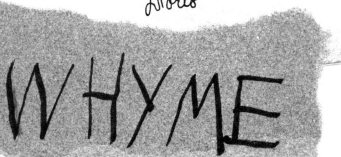

Helping Families Cope

Remember there are others who also hurt, such as grandparents.

Don't overreact. Rage is often dumped on friends.

Be sympathetic with parents who receive insensitive remarks.

Parents need a "fan club" to encourage them. Tell them they are doing a great job.

Recognize that parents and children need to deny the seriousness of the illness at times.

Help with parenting. Parents of young children with cancer may be quite young.

Listen as parents share their feelings. Don't correct. Just listen.

Stay with the child at the hospital while the parents go home to rest.

Follow the routine of the parents and hospital. Children feel safer with a known routine.

Help parents keep records in one place: tests, drugs, doctors' names. This information will be requested often.

Don't expect that what a parent says one time will be what is said another.

Hi my name is Katy and I found out I had leukemia and I had kemotherpy. My hair fell out and I was bald. It is not fun to be 10 years old and bald.

My Mother said my tumer is gone now. I was in the hospital but I still had to go to school but it was with a teacher who came to the hospital. I don't think it is fair when your sick and still have to go to school.
Ricky

Raol
110
Nen

My friend Jose just died from cansur. I'm only 9 years old and even I know that god has some special powers. why couldn't god stop Jose from dieing and make him well.

Raol

Katy

my docter

LOVE USA 25

Heart to Heart

Dear Katy,

I am so glad you wrote, but I'm very sorry that you got leukemia and had to have chemotherapy. I know the medicine is given to help you, but it doesn't make it easy to lose all your hair! Some kids say it helps to remember that their hair will grow back, and that losing your hair shows how strong the medicine is. Most kids wear fun hats or scarfs while their hair is growing back. I bet you have some nice ones, too. No matter how cute your scarfs are, though, it doesn't mean that you would like losing your hair! Nobody would want to be bald when they are ten years old, even for a short time. I am so glad that you told me how you feel. It helped to know what this is like for you.

Lots of love,

Anya

Heart to Heart

Dear Ricky,

I am so happy your tumor is gone now. Did you have an operation? You said you have school at the hospital with the special teacher and that that doesn't seem fair. There must be lots of things that don't seem fair about having a tumor and being in the hospital. One of the hardest things is that you don't have a choice about some of the things that happen to you.

Sometimes it helps to make choices about the things you can control: what to watch on TV, which homework to do first, what clothes to wear while you are in the hospital. I'm going to send you a giant hug in the mail and hope that you feel better really soon so you can go back to your regular school.

Love from your friend,

with love from anya

"Here To Stay"
BEING ADOPTED

Talking To Children About Adoption

The adoptive parents should be the ones to tell the children they are adopted.

Use the word *adopted* with the child even before it can be understood.

Offer a simple explanation of the adoption by the time the child is three or four years old.

Children who are told about their adoption when they are young still ask many questions when they are ten to twelve years old.

When talking about the adoption in the child's presence, give only information the child has been told.

Accept the child's need to find the birth parents.

Give the child information about searching for his birth parents, e.g., tell the child they may not want to be "found."

Tell children they can tell anyone they choose about the adoption.

When children are punished, they sometimes say, "You're not my real mother." The child can be told, "You really are our child because we legally adopted you."

Save details about the adoption for the child and let the child decide whether or not they should be shared.

I want to know all about my birth parents and I wonder if they are trying to find me. Sometimes I pretend they are RICH and FAMUS and live in a manshun and have a biltin pool.

Your friend,
Jonathan

I know my brothers and me were adopted but I love my parents and I don't care if they arn't real.

ME

DANA 6   TROY 8   BOBBY 2

Dear Jonathan,

You have been thinking lots about your birth parents. Many children wonder about their birth parents and sometimes pretend they are famous or rich. It is natural to wonder. Sometimes when kids are having a hard time with a problem at home, they imagine their parents are someone other than who they probably really are. Although it is fun to pretend, it is good to remember that these are only make-believe thoughts. Most kids find that it helps them most to accept the real world where they live and the real parents they have.

You asked another important question. Are your birth parents trying to find you? I don't know the answer to that question. I do know that other children wonder about the same thing after they have been adopted. It may help you to talk about all of these questions with your parents. They may have information that would answer some of your questions. Thanks for writing, Jonathan!

Love,

Doris

Heart to Heart

Dear Troy,

I just loved your letter! I think your letter would make your parents very happy! I'm glad that you and your brothers were adopted by parents that love you so much and I know for sure they are glad they have three wonderful boys that love them! You said you love them even if they aren't "real," but dear Troy, they couldn't be more real if they had given birth to you. You are very lucky boys and they are very lucky parents and you have a real family.

Hugs,

Doris

Answering Questions

"Why did they give me up?"

For reasons beyond their control. I don't know, but it must have been very hard to part with you.

"What kind of people were my birth parents?"

They were good people who wanted the best for you. They were probably like us.

"What do you know about my birth parents?"

I've heard they liked music and were nice looking, like you.

"How did you choose me?"

We told the people at the adoption agency about the kind of baby we wanted and they found you for us.

"Why didn't you have a real baby?"

Adoption means you are our real child. You didn't grow inside Mommy, but that isn't what makes you our child forever.

"Were my birth parents criminals?"

Your parents were very young when you were born, and they did not know how to take care of you. They were not criminals.

"Does my mother miss me?"

I'm sure she does at times.

How Children Feel

Most children feel they are part of the adoptive family and "forget" they were adopted. This is especially true if they were adopted at birth.

Some children feel "special" because they were adopted and specifically wanted. Others feel insecure and worry that the adoptive family won't keep them. They sometimes worry about whether they will "be adequate" to satisfy the adoptive parents.

Each child is unique and feels differently. Here's a list of possible ways children might feel about being adopted:

♡ confused, resentful, and embarrassed in addition to feeling loved and grateful.

♡ sad. Any child available for adoption has lost his birth parents in some way.

♡ insecure that they have less status than birth children in the home.

♡ defensive or protective of their birth parents.

♡ responsible for the need of adoption; i.e., "I was a bad kid, therefore my parents put me up for adoption."

♡ lonely; that they don't really belong. Their heritage is unknown.

♡ anxious about their birth parents' safety, health, and happiness.

♡ angry and hurt that their birth parents allowed the adoption.

I was adopted when I was a baby at the hospital. I don't know what my birth mother looked like but I hope I can see her some day. I don't want to go with her I just want to see her.

Cathy

My name is Barbara Ann. My little sister is not adopted, but I am. My parents said they couldn't have a baby so they adopted me, then all of a sudden BIG SURPRISE! I liked it better when it was just me.

Anya 8

Dear Cathy,

You didn't say how old you are now, Cathy, but lots of kids who were adopted when they were babies are curious to know more about their birth parents as they get older. It's okay to wonder what your mother looked like, and I do understand that you don't mean that you want to go with her. I don't know if this will be possible because some birth parents can't be found, and others choose not to see their birth children because they have made new lives for themselves.

But you can tell your parents how you feel and see what they say. It is scary for parents to encourage their children to find their birth parents because they don't want to see their loved children hurt, and that can happen. Sometimes kids just imagine what their parents might look like because they probably look something like you!

Much love,

Doris

Dear Barbara Ann,

I'm glad you told me about your little sister and I can understand that it is hard when you have been the only child and now your parents give some of their attention to the new baby. It is also hard for some adopted kids because they worry that their parents might love their birth baby more than they love them.

Love is something that grows in your heart and doesn't come automatically by being a birth child. My guess is that your parents love you very much and are glad that you are their first child. No one can ever take your place in their hearts. You will always be the oldest and you will always be as much their child as this new baby.

When you were tiny your parents had to take a lot of time to take care of you, and now they will do that for your new sister. What are some of the things that you can do because you are the oldest that the baby can't do?

Lots of Love,

Doris

What to Do

Each time the adoption is discussed with the child there should be lots of smiles, hugs, and pleasure.

Support the adoptive parents. Many have never parented a child before.

Expect the child to make a successful adjustment and be matter of fact about problems.

Encourage children to talk about what they are thinking and feeling.

Provide books about other children who have been adopted.

Help children from other cultures maintain ties to their heritage.

Help the child feel more included in the family by developing traditions, especially around holidays.

Asking for a medical history from the birth parents will be helpful to the child later.

Feelings of attachment don't come automatically. Hugging, holding, touching, and playing with the child help.

When the child first arrives, limit the number of visitors until he has had time to adjust.

Don't tell the child more about the adoption than is asked.

Never jokingly say, "You've been so bad lately we'll have to send you back to the agency."

What to Avoid

Don't refer to the birth parents as the "real parents."

Don't tell children they were "put up for adoption."

Don't say or imply that only "bad things" come from being adopted.

Don't tell children that if they hadn't been adopted they'd still be in a foster home.

Don't expect the child to be always "grateful."

Don't leave the child unprepared to answer insensitive questions at school: "Didn't your parents want you?"

Don't compare biological children with adopted children in the family.

Don't feel that a child's search for his heritage reflects on the love for the adoptive parents.

Don't introduce the child as an "adopted child."

Don't expect adoption to erase years of hurt and rejection that might have occurred prior to the adoption.

Don't expect all of the issues about the adoption to be apparent initially for the older child.

Don't minimize the child's adjustment to a new value system at the adoptive parents' home.

I don't know what to do on Mothers Day. My birth Mother will come to see me but I don't want my Mom to get her feelings hurt if I make two Mothers Day cards please help me.   Crystal

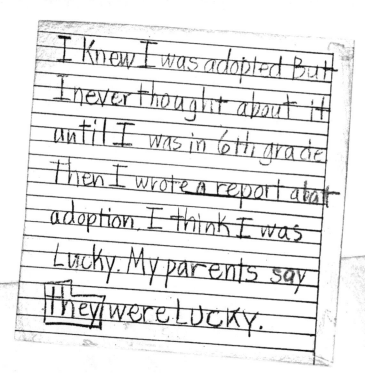

I Knew I was adopted But I never thought about it until I was in 6th grade then I wrote a report about adoption. I think I was lucky. My parents say they were Lucky.

Dear Crystal,

What a thoughtful girl you are to be concerned about how your mom will feel if you gave a Mother's Day card to your birth mother, too! One thing you could do is make two very different cards and you could write a special love note inside the card for your mom so it would feel extra special. Being a mother is more than just giving birth, so although you have a "birth mother" and an "adoptive mother," the mother who has taken care of you is your mother now.

It sounds like you have an on-going relationship with your birth mother because of an "open adoption." I'm sure you have special warm feelings for her. I can understand wanting to give both of them a card. You are a sensitive, caring girl!

Love,
Doris

Heart to Heart INC

General Guidelines

You should know that . . .

♡ if children are not adopted at birth they will need help in grieving the losses of the important people in their lives.

♡ loss of former significant adults often means the loss of self identity and worth.

♡ children need permission to talk about their birth parents without fear of hurting their adoptive parents' feelings.

♡ they develop fantasies about their parents and may describe them as saints they never were. Be gentle in presenting reality.

♡ they think far more about their adoption than adoptive parents know.

♡ when children are "chosen" because they were "cute" or "so good" they may feel they will be "unchosen" when these qualities are lacking.

♡ children wonder if they have brothers or sisters they don't know about. They wonder if their birth parents think about them and miss them.

♡ it helps to honor anniversaries as important events; i.e., celebrate "adoption day."

♡ Mother's Day is sometimes a difficult day for adopted children.

♡ children must be told again and again about the adoption. Telling is not a one-time event.

"Shamed and Blamed"
KEEPING THE SECRET OF SEXUAL ABUSE

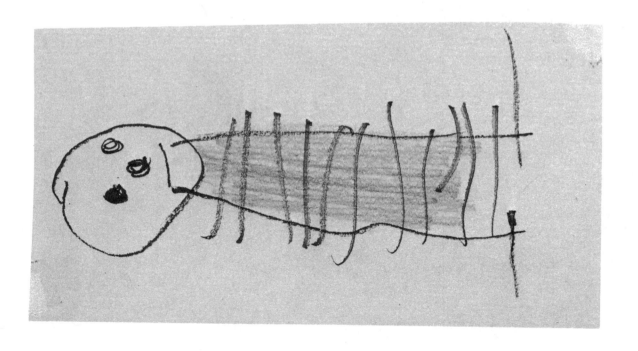

Clues of Abuse

What is Sexual Abuse?

It includes a wide range of behaviors including adult nudity, intimate kissing, sexual touch, penetration, and pornography.

Abuse is usually gradual and progressive. It often begins with inappropriate touch before it is clearly sexual.

Sexual abuse is common. One of three girls and one of seven boys will be abused before the age of eighteen.

Vulnerable children are loners, are physically underdeveloped for their age, and have low self-esteem.

Sexual abuse often begins when the child is eight years old.

The average child makes nine attempts to disclose the abuse before someone responds. Boys often have more trouble than girls in saying they have been abused.

Here are some "clues" given by children who have been abused:

♡   not wanting to spend time with an adult known by the family.
♡   unusual shyness about the body.
♡   extreme change in behavior, such as change in appetite or particular fears.
♡   unusual knowledge about sex or reenactments of sexual behaviors.
♡   expressing affection inappropriately.
♡   physical complaints such as tummy aches, nightmares, restlessness, and bed-wetting.

Dear friend,

I still haven't told my parents about what happened to me. The man who did this to me is very old. If I told he might go to jail. I think that I can forget about this until he dies. I'll be glad and able to live the rest of my life in peace.

Love,

Joe

P.S. I hope he doesn't go to Heaven because I want to go there.

Dear Friend Joe,

Thanks for writing again, Joe. It was good to hear from you and know what you are thinking and feeling. It seems to me you have thought carefully about whether to disclose the abuse to your parents and that you feel it wouldn't be worth the guilty feelings you would have if the man is punished. If the abuse was still occurring, I would encourage you more strongly to tell your parents. I think it is important for you to ask this question: Do I want to avoid telling what happened because I don't feel worthy of getting him in trouble? Do I feel that it's better for me to suffer than for him? (So many of the kids who write to us have damaged feelings of self-worth and don't feel they deserve to expose someone else.)

Maybe there will come a time when you feel comfortable sharing what happened. Remember, you were completely innocent. It was all his responsibility. In the meantime I pray you will know more how precious and loved you are.

Your friend,

Doris

Dear Heart to Heart
Thank you for that Book (I Cant talk About It) Because I was abuse. when I was 8½ to 9½ and did not know if I should tell or not it was very hard. ther is some thing still bothering me inside. Thank you for that book I really needed to read it.

love,
Jennifer

♡ masturbation, which may result in further rejection.

♡ unprovoked anger expressed at things or people other than the abuser.

Note: A child who is being sexually abused may show no visible signs until much later in life.

Traits of Abusers and Abusive Homes

Both men and women abuse children.

Sexual abuse occurs in any social, religious, or economic class and in any race.

Abusive fathers may be overly protective of a favorite child.

Some abusive fathers are strict authoritarians.

Abusive homes often have inappropriate sleeping arrangements.

Offenders frequently tell children, "Your mom knows about this and said it is OK."

Mothers may be present in the home during abuse, but "tune it out."

An abusing parent often has low self-esteem and feels unable to get needs met in a mature way.

Abusers usually abuse repeatedly with other children.

Abuse usually occurs in the child's or the offender's home.

Children are often gradually seduced by gifts, attention, and favors.

AMY

Love Dove

Dear, Doris my name is Donna and My mom got married I was scared of my step-father. very much and one day he raped me. I read your book it made me cry. I'm nine years old. He's in jail right now because he threatened my mom with a gun. I hope to go to court and I'm scared. I wish I could talk to someone a nice as Love Dove.
Sincerely,
Donna
P.S. Please wright back thank you.

Heart to Heart

Dear sweet Donna,

I'm so glad you wrote to say you don't have to go to court because your stepdad admitted everything! You also talked about how very, very sad you feel because of what happened to you. I'm sure it must make you feel angry, too. God knows all about those hurt, scared, angry, sad feelings. He is like "Love-Dove" in our book *I Can't Talk about It*. I know God was hurt and sad because you—His very special, loved, and precious child—were not treated as you deserve.

You said you will hate your stepdad forever. I don't blame you for feeling that way, honey. God knows you have a right to feel angry and He never pushes us to forgive before we are ready. Someday, you may hate him less, and when that happens there will be more room in your heart for love. God will help you do this, but for now, you need to let all that hurt and pain out, and not cover it up by pretending everything is OK, when it's not OK! Some of God's best friends in the Bible were people who were very angry about other people hurting them. God understood.

I prayed for you today.

Hugs,

Doris

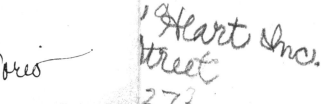

NICK

JOEL

If You Discover Abuse

Tell children that:

♡ you believe what they have told you.

♡ they did the right thing in telling you and that you will help.

♡ you need to tell certain adults who can protect them so the abuse will stop.

Remain outwardly calm. Visible shock may be interpreted as feelings about the child.

Call the State Children's Protective Services and report the abuse. If you are not sure if the abuse occurred, trust your instincts and notify authorities.

Be careful who you tell and don't talk about it in the child's presence.

Don't ask for lengthy details because all of this will have to be repeated to the authorities.

Don't send children home after they have disclosed the abuse because they may feel guilty and change the story to cover up for the abuser.

Don't call the parents and tell them what you know. Let the professionals do this.

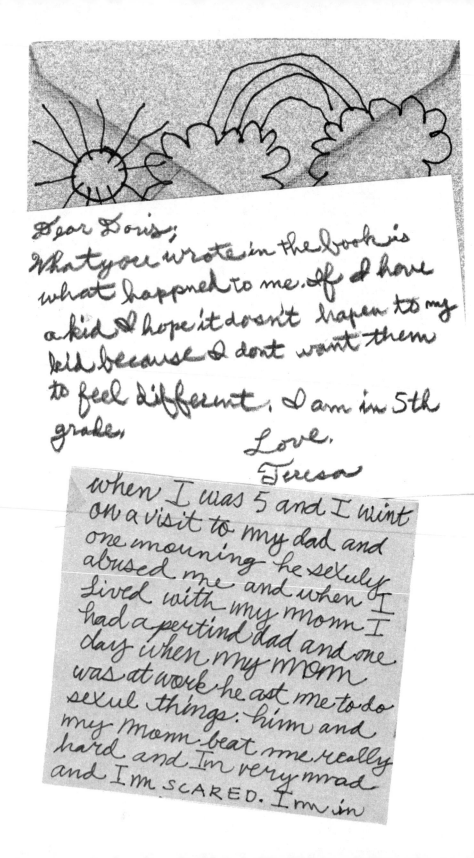

Dear Doris;

What you wrote in the book is what happened to me. If I have a kid I hope it dosn't hapen to my kid because I dont want them to feel different. I am in 5th grade,

Love,
Teresa

when I was 5 and I wint on a visit to my dad and one mouning he sexulf abused me and when I lived with my mom I had a pertind dad and one day when my mom was at work he ast me to do sexul things: him and my mom beat me really hard and I'm very mrad and I'm SCARED. I'm in

Hart to Hart

The Book "I CAN'T TALK ABOUT IT" Is what hapend to me. By the way my name is Marty. I am in Fith grade. I Like your Book. I Love your pictures. It is exactly what hapend to me when I lived with my step Dad.

Pleasa send any more stories or information that you have that will help me.

LOVE,
Marty

How Children Feel

Confused:

♡ by "the morning after," since the abuser acts as if nothing unusual has occurred.

♡ by the unknown language, e.g., "abused," "court date," "victim," "offender."

♡ by statements that imply the abuse is for their own good: "Daddy wants you to know what sex is about."

Guilty. Since they are rarely forced to participate, they feel responsible for the abuse: "I made my Daddy do this." This is reinforced when the parents blame them for "allowing" the abuse.

Ashamed. The child feels dirty, worthless, alone, and different.

Afraid:

♡ they will "lose their daddy's love."

♡ the family will break up.

♡ no one will believe them.

♡ they will be removed from the home.

Invalidated. Some children are told not to talk about the abuse any further: "We'll work this out in the family," or "Daddy said he wouldn't do it anymore."

Helping Children Cope

Let them tell the story many times.

Don't try to determine the degree of harm done.

Get professional help. The shamed family will have a hard time acknowledging the need.

Don't be afraid to hug and hold the child.

Teach children they have the right to say "no" to any touch they don't want, and the differences between a good touch and a bad touch.

If you have been sexually abused, allow the child to respond differently than you did.

It is not necessary for the child to confront the person who abused him. He may be reabused in that meeting.

Don't assume that because the abuser apologized he/she will stop abusing. This is almost never the case. Abusers must have treatment.

Don't underestimate the potential for healing the emotional damage to the child.

Tell them:

♡ it was not their fault, even though they may have liked the special attention. Say, "The adult is to blame for this."

♡ the body responds automatically and that does not mean they liked the abuse.

Note: Children's responses to sexual abuse are influenced by the adults who surround the child. If we see abused children as "damaged," they will pick up on that.

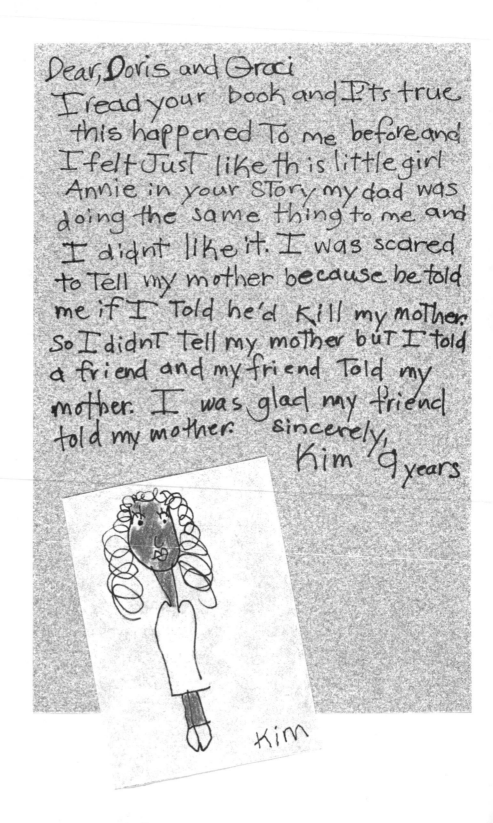

Dear, Doris and Graci
I read your book and It's true this happened To me before and I felt Just like this little girl Annie in your Story my dad was doing the same thing to me and I didn't like it. I was scared to Tell my mother because he told me if I Told he'd Kill my mother. So I didn't Tell my mother but I told a friend and my friend Told my mother. I was glad my friend told my mother. sincerely, Kim 9 years

Kim

Dear Kim,

I felt so sad when I read your letter. You are a precious little girl and deserve to be protected and not hurt by the people you trusted. It must have been very scary to hear your dad say that he would kill your mother if you told about the abuse. That is one way for you to know that what he was doing was very wrong. He wouldn't have had to cover it up if his actions were okay.

You were brave and strong and wise to tell your friend. It is the only way to make the abuse stop. I think you have a special friend who loves you enough to want to help you! Honey, your daddy may never admit that he was doing wrong things and hurting you, but you know that he was wrong. You can begin to feel better now that the abuse has stopped. One of the ways to help yourself is to talk about your feelings with a safe adult, like the school counselor or a play therapist. I am praying for you today, dear Kim.

Much love and prayers,

Doris

Innocent Child

Precious One
I know you've been sad for so long
Don't blame yourself
You didn't do anything wrong
You only wanted approval
Every child needs the same
You are as pure as a flower
in the cleansing rain

It's not your fault
You are an innocent child
It's not your fault
You are an innocent child

Precious One
I know the nightmares you've had
Don't be ashamed
You didn't do anything bad
You only wanted attention
Every child needs love
You are a perfect creation
of God above

It's not your fault
You are an innocent child
It's not your fault
You are an innocent child[1]

Steve Siler

Note
1. Steve Siler, *Innocent Child*, (Fifty States Music, 1989). Used by permission. Taken from the audio cassette of *I Can't Talk about It* (Portland, Ore.: Multnomah Press, 1986). This cassette contains gentle songs written for young children who have been abused.

I'm a survivor of sex abuse by my older brother. It has taken me 13 years to remember what happened. Would you please send me information on God's love? It's hard to believe God could really love me.

Dear Doris and Graci,
At 37, I may be older than your intended audience for your book I CAN'T TALK ABOUT IT.
My therapist gave it to me to get in touch with the little girl inside me who was abused by her Dad.

The end of the book with emphasis on forgiveness and God's love really touched me. God has been the basis of my healing. Eventually I would like to [use] my experience and training [to help] other women in [...]

❀ ❀ Marla ♡

Dear Doris,
I wanted to write you about your book "I Can't Talk About It" that I read recently. I am a grown woman who has just begun to deal with my childhood incest and other abuse. A good friend shared her book with me. It made me cry that I did not have a book like that when I was a child, but it is very important to me now. I took the book to my counselor. She says I have multiple personalities. When one of them is frightened, the counselor reads to her and she feels better.
She tells me I have a very long way to go, but I just look at the pictures in your book and have courage.
Thank you for writing to help me with my fears and memories.

Marla
[...] Desert
AZ

Heart to Heart
[...]

PHOENIX
AZ
30
[...]

Greetings
USA

Heart to Heart

Dear Marla,

Thank you for your letter and for sharing a little of your journey. I'm sure your early abuse has deeply touched your life, and I also know how very much work it is to face the past and move beyond the pain. Our hearts and love and prayers are with you.

Of course it is difficult for you to feel God's love for you when you have been wounded so much by your earthly father. Fortunately, God's love is not dependent on our feelings. I believe he hurt with you—his precious, loved child—each time your father abused you. He also knows, dear Marla, that you are healthy in many areas of your life and that you have the ability to heal and grow and to walk away from your past, a whole person.

It has been my observation that for most women the freedom to accept the tender loving heavenly Father is dependent on trusting Him enough to know He can handle your rage. You don't have to stuff your feelings. He knows it all, anyway. I love the quote from Phillips Brooks, "The only way to get rid of your past is to get a future out of it." God is there. And He loves you.

Our hearts and love and prayers are with you for your journey ahead, Marla. Some day you will be on the other side of your pain.

Love,

What About Forgiveness?

Forgiveness is a slow, deliberate process and should not be pushed. It will need to be addressed again and again.

Letting go of the past does not depend on the acknowledgement of abuse by the abuser.

The core of forgiveness is to see the abuser as a wounded, sinful person whom God loves as much as he loves the abused person.

Forgiveness is not denying or minimizing the abuse.

Long Term Fall Out

The fallout from sexual abuse lingers long after the abuse has stopped. Many of the letters we have received are from adults—grown up on the outside, but wounded children inside. The work of healing can begin at ANY point.

Trust has been broken in an abusive relationship. This is the ultimate betrayal. Adults abused as children may:

♡   have difficulty trusting others and developing intimacy.

♡   experience anger, depression, low self-esteem, and have difficulty with sexual relationships.

♡   submerged memories resurface late in life when the adult is ready to remember. When these memories surface, they are usually vague at first.

Burying the past is like holding a beach ball under water. It works—but not for long.

AFTER THE FACT

Survivors, Not Victims

When I speak to adults I often ask, "How many of you had a good childhood?" Some raise their hands, but most don't. When I ask, "Who are you today in relationship to that pain?" most say they were forced to find honest answers from God, drop their masks, and become more real. They are not perfect or unscathed, but they are stronger, more authentic, and committed to helping others.

Lifelong emotional disability does not have to follow early childhood trauma. I believe that all of us—no matter our age or our pain—have been provided the opportunity to grow and to become emotionally and spiritually sturdy.

I don't believe that experiences themselves "make or break" us. The same water that hardens an egg softens a carrot. If we long for what never was and never can be, we become a hostage of the past. We can either choose to become bitter, isolated, and hostile or we can choose to grow. Growth comes with saying goodbye to the wish for a perfect past and welcoming the reality of the present.

It isn't easy. The healing process is usually slow and filled with hard emotional work. But the result is freedom . . . and freedom is worth emotional sweat!

If you have experienced childhood pain, hang in there. Life can be better! What is crucial to our ability to grow and become strong is our response to those circumstances—and the support that surrounds us.

One loving adult with an enduring, stubborn, irrational commitment to a child can make the difference between emotional life or death for that child. We must never minimize the profound importance to a child of a long-term loving relationship with an adult. Professional technique cannot replace love. The child may need professional play therapy, but that will not be a substitute for the loving presence of an adult friend. Right technique is not nearly as important as a right relationship with the child.

Children select the adults who merit their trust. The question is not what we say to them, but how we feel about them. Children will hear how we feel, and respond accordingly.

Children who have been repeatedly hurt by adults have no reason to assume that other adults will treat them any differently. The only way they can know safety with an adult is through time. Adults who give up quickly will miss the payoff of investment in the child.

When God wants to hug a child He sends someone to put His arms around him. We can always think of someone who would be better at helping . . . if only they were available.

An old Chinese proverb says that each child is a piece of paper and every passerby leaves his mark. There is no higher calling than to leave the mark of love on a child. "Whoever receives one of these little ones in my name, receives Me."

I like to hear children
when they talk and play.
They splatter all their
words around and
sprinkle up the place.
by
Melody   age 7

Love

haha
ha

I   Like   to   Play

Dear Doris,
Thank you for Helping me throw my parents divorce. I realy apresheated the help. Thanks for being ther for me when I needd someone to talk or write a leter to a speisle friend. Thanks alot

Your old friend, PELE.

PS sorry for saying thanks So late

Sincerely →
PELE

to Haert s Street 1222

KOKOMO, IN 459

bad →

good

I love you Grandma. AE

Encouragement for Comforters

If you give yourself to the hungry, and satisfy the desire of the afflicted, then your light will rise in darkness, and your gloom will become like midday (Isaiah 58:10, NASB).

Now go ahead and do as I tell you, for I will help you to speak well, and I will tell you what to say (Exodus 4:15, TLB).

And let us not be weary in well doing: for in due season we shall reap, if we faint not (Galatians 6:9, KJV).

Fear not, for I am with you, so do not be dismayed. I am your God. I will strengthen you: I will help you: I will uphold you with my victorious right hand (Isaiah 41:10, TLB).

If any one serves me, let him follow me: and where I am, there shall my servants also be; if any one serves me, the Father will honor him (John 12:26, NASB).

If anyone so much as gives you a cup of water because you are Christ's—I say solemnly—he won't lose his reward (Mark 9:41).

He will shield you with his wings! They will shelter you. His faithful promises are your armor (Psalm 91:4).

I will instruct you and teach you in the way which you should go. I will counsel you with my eye upon you (Psalm 32:8, NASB).

The Lord has anointed me to bring good news to the suffering and afflicted. He has sent me to comfort the broken-hearted, to announce liberty to captives and to open the eyes of the blind. He has sent me to tell those who mourn that the time of God's favor to them has come. To all who mourn in Israel he will give: Beauty for ashes; joy instead of mourning; praise instead of heaviness (Isaiah 61:1-3, TLB).

MATT